Art and Institution

AT
MEDWAY
LIBRARY

D1425093

Bloomsbury Studies in Continental Philosophy
Series Editor: James Fieser, University of Tennessee at Martin, USA

Bloomsbury Studies in Continental Philosophy is a major monograph series from Bloomsbury. The series features first-class scholarly research monographs across the field of Continental philosophy. Each work makes a major contribution to the field of philosophical research.

Adorno's Concept of Life, Alastair Morgan
Being and Number in Heidegger's Thought, Michael Roubach
Badiou, Marion and St Paul, Adam Miller
Deleuze and Guattari, Fadi Abou-Rihan
Deleuze and the Genesis of Representation, Joe Hughes
Deleuze and the Unconscious, Christian Kerslake
Deleuze, Guattari and the Production of the New, edited by Simon O'Sullivan and
    Stephen Zepke
Derrida, Simon Morgan Wortham
Derrida and Disinterest, Sean Gaston
Derrida: Profanations, Patrick O'Connor
Encountering Derrida, edited by Simon Morgan Wortham and Allison Weiner
The Domestication of Derrida, Lorenzo Fabbri
Foucault's Heidegger, Timothy Rayner
Gadamer and the Question of the Divine, Walter Lammi
Heidegger and a Metaphysics of Feeling, Sharin N. Elkholy
Heidegger and Aristotle, Michael Bowler
Heidegger and Logic, Greg Shirley
Heidegger and Philosophical Atheology, Peter S. Dillard
Heidegger Beyond Deconstruction, Michael Lewis
Heidegger, Politics and Climate Change, Ruth Irwin
Heidegger's Early Philosophy, James Luchte
Kant, Deleuze and Architectonics, Edward Willatt
Levinas and Camus, Tal Sessler
Merleau-Ponty's Phenomenology, Kirk M. Besmer
Nietzsche's Ethical Theory, Craig Dove
Nietzsche, Nihilism and the Philosophy of the Future, edited by Jeffrey Metzger
Place, Commonality and Judgment, Andrew Benjamin
Sartre's Phenomenology, David Reisman
Nietzsche's Thus Spoke Zarathustra, edited by James Luchte
Time and Becoming in Nietzsche's Thought, Robin Small
The Philosophy of Exaggeration, Alexander Garcia Düttmann
Who's Afraid of Deleuze and Guattari? Gregg Lambert
Žižek and Heidegger, Thomas Brockelman

Art and Institution

Aesthetics in the Late Works of Merleau-Ponty

Rajiv Kaushik

B L O O M S B U R Y
LONDON • NEW DELHI • NEW YORK • SYDNEY

Bloomsbury Academic
An imprint of Bloomsbury Publishing Plc

50 Bedford Square
London
WC1B 3DP
UK

175 Fifth Avenue
New York
NY 10010
USA

www.bloomsbury.com

First published by Continuum International Publishing Group 2011
Paperback edition first published 2013

© Rajiv Kaushik, 2011

All rights reserved. No part of this publication may be reproduced or transmitted in
any form or by any means, electronic or mechanical, including photocopying,
recording, or any information storage or retrieval system, without prior permission in
writing from the publishers.

Rajiv Kaushik has asserted his right under the Copyright, Designs and Patents Act,
1988, to be identified as Author of this work.

No responsibility for loss caused to any individual or organization acting on or
refraining from action as a result of the material in this publication can be accepted
by Bloomsbury Academic or the author.

British Library Cataloguing-in-Publication Data
A catalogue record for this book is available from the British Library.

ISBN: HB: 978-1-4411-3663-3
PB: 978-0-5675-9248-4

Library of Congress Cataloging-in-Publication Data
Kaushik, Rajiv.
Art and institution: aesthetics in the late works of Merleau-Ponty / Rajiv Kaushik.
p. cm.
ISBN: 978-1-4411-3663-3
1. Merleau-Ponty, Maurice, 1908–1961. 2. Aesthetics. I. Title. II. Title:
Aesthetics in the late works of Merleau-Ponty.
B2430.M3764K38 2011
111'.85092–dc22
2010032996

Typeset by Newgen Imaging Systems Pvt Ltd, Chennai, India

For my wife, Natalie

Contents

List of Abbreviations   viii

Introduction   1
Chapter 1   Matisse in Slow Motion   28
Chapter 2   Art and Natural Being   59
Chapter 3   Proust and the Significant Event   91
Chapter 4   A Figurative Dimension: Reversibility
                    Between the Arts   112
Concluding Remarks   131

Notes   139
Bibliography   156
Index   161

Abbreviations

EM   Heidegger, Martin (1953) *Einführung in die Metaphysik*. Tübingen: Niemeyer.

GA   Heidegger, Martin (1975) *Gesamtausgabe* vol. 9, entitled *Wegmarken*, edited by Friedrich-wilhelm von Herrmann. Franfkfurt am Main: Vittorio Klostermann.

HLP   Maurice Merleau-Ponty, *Husserl at the Limits of Phenomenology*, edited by Leonard Lawlor and Bettina Bergo. Evanston: Northwestern University.

IP   Merleau-Ponty, Maurice (2003). *L'institution, La passivité: Notes de cours au Collège de France*. Paris: Editions Belin.

IPP   Merleau-Ponty, Maurice (1970) *In Praise of Philosophy and Other Essays*, translated by John O'Neill. Evanston: Northwestern University Press.

N   Merleau-Ponty, Maurice (2003) *Nature: Course Notes from the Collège de France*, translated by Robert Vallier. Evanston: Northwestern University Press.

PP   Merleau-Ponty (2003) Maurice *Phenomenology of Perception*, translated by Colin Smith. London: Routledge Press.

PrP   Merleau-Ponty, Maurice (1964) *Primacy of Perception and Other Essays*, edited by James E. Edie. Evanston: Northwestern University Press.

PW   Merleau-Ponty, Maurice (1973) *Prose of the World*, translated by John O'Neill. Evanston: Northwestern University Press.

S   Merleau-Ponty, Maurice (1964) *Signs*, translated by Richard C. McCleary. Evanston: Northwestern University Press.

SNS Merleau-Ponty, Maurice (1964) *Sense and Nonsense*, translated by Hubert L. Dreyfus and Patricia Allen Dreyfus. Evanston: Northwestern University Press.

VI Merleau-Ponty, Maurice (1968) *The Visible and the Invisible*, translated by Alphonso Lingis. Evanston: Northwestern University Press.

"Ursprung" Husserl, Edmund (1940) "Grundlegende Untersuchungen zum phänomologischen Ursprung der Räumlichkeit der Natur" in *Philosophical Essays in Memory of Edmund Husserl*. Cambridge: Harvard University Press.

Introduction

The title of this work is *Art and Institution: Aesthetics in the Late Works of Merleau-Ponty*. It is not an historical analysis of Merleau-Ponty's thought as it develops from his early period to his later period. The aim of this work is not to mark something like a "turn" in his writings on art that distinguishes one stage of development from another. Nor is its aim, on the contrary, to show that Merleau-Ponty's early essays and commentaries on the work of art are already pregnant with the themes of his later essays and commentaries. This book does not concern itself, at least not as a central focus, with the historical question of relation between Merleau-Ponty's various texts. It begins with Merleau-Ponty's more explicit adoption of the notion of "institution" or "primal-institution" (*Stiftung* or *UrStiftung*) and takes up the specific themes that follow therefrom and are characteristic of his later works. This book, then, is primarily concerned with the period ranging from 1952, with the publication of the second instalment of "Indirect Language and the Voices of Silence" in *Les Temps Modernes*, which would also appear later in *Signs*,[1] to 1961, at the time of his death in the midst of writing *The Visible and the Invisible*.[2]

Art and Institution focuses on "institution" (a primal foundation, initiation, establishment) as it relates to art. Institution is a notion first introduced by Husserl and later adopted by Merleau-Ponty to describe the appearing of the appearance as prior to both subjectivity and objectivity, and thus possessing a generative force that is irreducible to cognition and to an objective order of events in time. The work of art, when it is viewed from within its own mode of being rather than from some theoretical hindsight that aims to explain it, is committed neither to the constructs of subjectivity nor to the systems of objectivity. In itself, it is rather uniquely self-referential such that it points back into its own origins, towards the apparitional power implicit in its own appearance.[3] In giving access to its own ground, then, the artwork does not refer to anything outside of itself at the same time that it betrays an inner-connection to the institution prior to subject and object. It is important to note that Merleau-Ponty's "aesthetics," in this context, does not appeal to some established conceptual framework. It does not indicate a new category of knowledge. The aesthetic indicates nothing less than a refined way of being of the artwork in which its own phenomenality shows itself from its own inside out and reveals what has instituted it. This is why Merleau-Ponty's concern with aesthetics is always with a sensitivity to the *work* of art that is as much the event of creation as it is the created object.

Far from being a restricted mode of access available only to the artist, for Merleau-Ponty this aesthetic contains something that in fact proves to be foundational to phenomenology. For if it discloses the very ground of its own appearing it is this ground to which the reflexivity of phenomenology must return in order to be a phenomenology. Where phenomenology takes up the task of uncovering the logic of experience from within that experience, of discovering the hitherto unthought conditions of possibility of experience from within that experience, the aesthetic will prove to disclose the very condition to which this phenomenology needs to return. In this sense the aesthetic, for Merleau-Ponty, may be ontologically prior to phenomenology, but the method of phenomenology is nevertheless a propaedeutic in the recuperation of the aesthetic in its original sense.

Art, Phenomenology, Dialectic

Phenomenology does not introduce a new system of aesthetics, but rather it *comes back* to the aesthetic. Phenomenology, that is, allows the work of art's own mode of being to appear, and it does so by tending to it on its own terms and without any previous notions applied to it. Thus the artwork, approached pheomenologically, does not give access to the structures of subjectivity as such. Nor does the work allow us to witness, from the distant vantage of a neutral and un-invested subject, the structures of objectivity as such. The artwork, for Merleau-Ponty, is not per se *reflective* of its own origins but rather, as *pre-reflective*, allows access to a way of being in which no distinction between subject and object has yet been made. The work of art is thus, in turn, intimately bound with institution. For institution is nothing less than the existent process prior to subject and object that makes their relation possible. This region of institution is that to which the rigorously reflective method of phenomenology will demand a return. In this sense, the artwork, and specifically the region of existence it inhabits and confers into the world, is antecedent or anterior to phenomenology – the unreflective side necessary to reflectivity.

I want to show that the artwork, in its connection with institution, allows us to think through the problems that characterize Merleau-Ponty's late philosophy: *the overcoming of ontological difference, the significant event, and the reversibility of flesh.* But before I can go on to discuss in greater detail the character of this primal institutional region inhabited and revealed by the work of art – institution as the overcoming of ontological difference, as a significant event, and as the reversibility of flesh – the relation between art and phenomenology first needs further examination here. Why is the unreflective inherent to art so vital to phenomenology? And in what way does the artwork disclose the unreflective for phenomenology?

It is of course true that, although the notion of institution may not have always been explicit in his thought, Merleau-Ponty's interest in the work of art's relation to phenomenology runs throughout his entire career. The classic essay "Cézanne's Doubt," for instance, is almost entirely concerned with Cézanne's life and his canvases in order to learn something about phenomenality in its brute appearing.[4] Cézanne paints Mont Ste-Victoire on different occasions, we learn in that essay, and were one to view all his canvases together one would gain the impression of a perceptual reservoir that has allowed for many viewings. Mont Ste-Victoire is seen from many different angles at once, sometimes from a distance, other times from within its midst. On each sighting, a viewer gathers, the mountain gives itself for the sake of a new visibility, each time articulating a new differential space to its viewer. There is apparently no end to these possible spacings – why could the mountain not be painted *ad infinitum?* – and the mountain has not yet finished its own process of disclosure. The mountain discloses itself from out of itself, reveals itself as appearing from out of its own activity of formation. It does so without making reference to any structure behind itself – no thing-itself, and no world other than the sensible one from which its meaning arises. Analytically, Mont Ste-Victoire may be seen from one point of view – the subject's point of view – but analysis arrives after a certain delay. Cézanne's obsession, according to Merleau-Ponty, is simply to reveal a vision that is from the beginning stretched out across the various spaces of the mountain's own disclosure, distributed across a more primal field of vision, wandering out into and inscribed in that field of appearing. Merleau-Ponty writes that, "[o]nly one emotion is possible for this painter – the feeling of strangeness – and only one lyricism – that of the continual rebirth of existence."[5] He is given up to the emergent phenomenon that continually arises from elsewhere. The painter accepts Octavio Paz' sentiment: "in the middle of an eye," the poet writes, the "moment scatters." He "stays and goes"; he is "a pause."[6]

In illuminating this pause, this delay, this scattering of vision into the moment of the phenomenon's indefatigable emergence, painting, according to Merleau-Ponty, is significant for phenomenology. The two are not merely analogous. Merleau-Ponty famously tells us in "Cézanne's Doubt" that they in fact "share the same task," that is, "remaining faithful to the phenomena" and "expressing what *exists*," "the lived perspective, that which we actually perceive."[7] The painter's fidelity to phenomena, for Merleau-Ponty, discloses a *logos* which inhabits the sensuous and which is known to us prior to any cognitive operation that determines objectivity. It discloses the "physiognomy of objects and faces," he says, an internal "vibration of appearances which is the cradle of things."[8]

Phenomenology, too, revisits the traditional problem of relation between a subject and an object by placing this relation – the relation of intentionality – at the very core of philosophical reflection. On the one hand, the analysis of intentionality reveals a subject in its transcendence, a subject that has its own intending structures over its object. On the other hand, this same analysis brings to the light of day an appearing of the object that is linked with the intention directed towards it. A rigorous reflection on intentionality is thus forced to enter a domain more primal than the two terms of its analysis. It goes beyond the subject's intentions of objects in order to discover an integrality that in fact appears prior to both terms. The subject, then, takes neither itself nor its object as absolute origination, until finally it discovers the hitherto unthematized identity that moves between what has been constituted and what is seen.

The rigorous interrogation of subjectivity thus inevitably involves its own destabilization, the uncovering of which forms the basic theme of Merleau-Ponty's phenomenology: a radical self-interrogation to discover the phenomenon's own possibilities and witness the birth of the origins of its own appearing. "The ultimate task of phenomenology as a philosophy of consciousness," Merleau-Ponty writes in "The Philosopher and His Shadow," "is to understand its relationship to non-phenomenology. What resists phenomenology within us – natural being . . ."[9] The recovery of an otherwise resistant natural being from within phenomenology does not mark a move away from an empirical thesis into a speculative antithesis. It does not require phenomenology to pass beyond itself and into a ground that is discovered only in conception. By natural being Merleau-Ponty rather indicates a genesis of sense that emerges from out of a *logos*, which has made itself available *in* the phenomenon. To say that phenomenology requires that we understand its relation to natural being is thus to say that, without speculation, phenomenology needs to recover, in the concrete, a fundamental openness to this implicit *logos*.

Referring to the retrieval of this concrete process of emergence in the phenomenon in *The Visible and the Invisible*, Merleau-Ponty describes what he calls a "hyper-dialectic." This dialectic is not a question of relation between two different terms that logically require each other, nor does it refer to a transcendent "third" that negotiates the two terms. Such definitions of dialectic require the importation of some supervenient logic to explain the phenomenon's coming-to-be from outside of its own emergence. Hyper-dialectic is, instead, what Merleau-Ponty calls a "good dialectic." It is a question of radical reflection that consists in being open to the particular phenomenon from within its own process of self-mediation, that is, being open to the very location in which the phenomenon itself arises and differentiates itself in experience. It is dialectic from within the concrete content.

In passing from phenomenology towards a natural being, then, phenomenology aims to discover the very process of differentiation that occurs in time and allows the articulated difference to appear from out of an alterior unifying ground in time.

It should be noted that phenomenology thereby returns to that which has already been restored in the work of art – the concrete logic of appearing in the phenomenon – and that the relation phenomenology discovers with artwork is itself hyper-dialectical. For it is with the work of art that phenomenology not only recovers an unreflective ground but also a ground from out of which reflectivity has differentiated itself. It is thus not only important that, as Merleau-Ponty notes, the work of art already "show[s] nature pure,"[10] and "suspends those habits of thought and reveals the base of inhuman nature upon which man has installed himself."[11] It is also key that the work of art shows the very region into which a phenomenology must pass in order to gain access to its own possibilities. That is, in disclosing an inhuman nature of the human, the artwork discloses the very ground into which phenomenology must pass in order to accomplish itself *as a phenomenology*.

If Merleau-Ponty understands the relation of phenomenology to art on the basis of this hyper-dialectic, and if art thus exposes the being to which phenomenology must return, then it is no doubt tempting to object that Merleau-Ponty simply subsumes the artwork under a general ontology and that he is in fact unable to let the work appear on its own terms. In this sense, it could be argued, art never conveys anything other than the ontological possibility for phenomenology, and thus it is in a deep sense de-aestheticized. Indeed Merleau-Ponty never seems to interrogate the artwork in its own being or concern himself with the problems that belong solely to it. The work of art, according to him, is always apparently subservient to the inner-logic of a vision that arises from out of a natural being. Merleau-Ponty's reference in "Eye and Mind" to painting as a "secret science" that is "further on," grounding a natural science, apparently corroborates this view.[12] For a *secret* science is especially important for Merleau-Ponty inasmuch as it founds all the sciences, though it is only phenomenology that remains attentive to this secret foundation.

Has not the history of painting itself shown that, at its core, painting in fact breaks with natural being and instead sides with a *pathos* that belongs to the artist apart from nature? The surrealist movement, as André Breton describes it in his now well-known manifesto, refuses to let an exterior reality reign over an interior reality, looking instead for a new super-reality that eventuates an imaginary scene of seemingly incongruent and apparently irrational events. Abstract expressionism is concerned with an inner-life of painting itself in the hopes of exposing the expressionistic gesture of the creative act, an act that is quite apart from the logic and norms of perspective and is even at times apparently derived from utter madness. James Elkins writes of "The Studio as a Kind of Psychosis," and the painter's paint creeping into every corner of the painter's life like the unconscious into every act.[13] But, for Merleau-Ponty, none of this really retrieves the radicality of the work of art itself, which is less about the subject's decision to create an art object. The original event of creation in fact resists the division between the *pathos* of art-working and natural being. The event happens from out of an ambivalence that bridges the distinction between the interiority and exteriority upon which a philosophy of art depends. There will be no solutions to the philosophical problems presented to us by a work of art, then, without any recovery of the originary ambivalence between interiority and an exteriority that grounds it, an ambivalence which Merleau-Ponty thinks is already inherent to the work. Thus Merleau-Ponty does not ever give an analysis of artwork without grounding it in being but, properly speaking, as I will explain a little further on, this does not mean that his ontology subsumes, and thus de-aestheticizes, the artwork.

No doubt Merleau-Ponty's insistence that the work of art brings into existence a fundamentally ambiguous line between interiority and exteriority runs counter to the western philosophy of art, which focuses either on the psychological conditions of the artist or the created object as distinct from the objects that it represents. But in fact, Merleau-Ponty might want to point out, the entire set of problems germane to the philosophy of the art trace back to a Greek ambivalence towards mimesis itself, and it is this basic ambivalence that is in need of recovering. The Greeks notice that the mimetic arts do not merely imply to copy, but also to imitate, indicate, suggest, express, represent. They thus also indicate a concentration of all the artist's organizational powers upon expression that is localized in the object being represented. This already requires an interpretation of experience, where this interpretation is determined by a mood hidden in expression that has infected the artist. There is a motive of representation, then, which may contain at least some reference to something original, whether this origin be fictional or real, but in doing so it can also produce a corresponding emotion: recognition, happiness, fear, respect, sorrow, despair, etc. The *motivation* to represent, for the Greeks, is what an objective philosophy must resist since it is precisely this motivation that takes us away from the real. But, where seeing *proper* is concerned, the Greeks also recognized an indirect quality, and consequently they believed in the possibility of a neutral apprehension of the objectivities by the seeing subject.[14] There is a link, according to them, between indirect perception and passivity: the pull of the eye into the landscape grants an all-important idea of a capacity for knowledge, a horizon of possible knowledge and things to know.[15] This leads to a specifically Greek sense of infinity that has to do with the contemplation of the invisible heavens and the extension of the eye into a philosophical wonder.[16]

The motivation to represent at first glance appears to do something to indirect and passive seeing. It seems to render this seeing in such a way that transforms it. But does this rendering turn vision into something other than what it is *in fact?* From where does the motivation to represent in terms of the visible arise if it differs from indirect seeing? We need to see how motivation and horizonality each have a condition of possibility in the other. This requires that our understanding of each term be deepened, not abandoned. The phenomenological sense of world refers to a more primal and as yet unthematized sense of the horizon of possible knowing, the horizon acting as the background in the formation of a world. The phenomenologically discovered world is the total nexus of relationships between actually presented objects, upon which consciousness acts, enacts and sees. It refers to familiarly encountered objects interrelated and ordered – near and far, lower and higher – and constituted within a spatial matrix that includes them. It also refers to the possibly presented objects, the objects upon which consciousness has yet to act, enact and see. It thus also includes objects as they appear ordered and extended in time (long ago, just now, in a while, yet to come), only to run off indefinitely into a horizon. The world, as it is uncovered in phenomenology, appears from out of a primordial openness. It requires a horizon in which potentiality is prefigured. The world, then, does not indicate an ideality but rather a set of occurring actualities that are in fact predelineated by potentially limitless modifications and augmentations of those actualities. These potentialities are concretely laid out before a consciousness prior to being thematized by that consciousness.

It is precisely this world of possibility, constantly operant in relation to whatever is now actually being presented, which is already evidenced by the painted world. Painting is, Merleau-Ponty writes in *The Visible and the Invisible*, a "world by opposition to the unique and 'real world' . . ."[17] In "Indirect Language and the Voices of Silence," Merleau-Ponty speaks of Renoir's "coherent deformation"[18] of the real scene, the "system of equivalences"[19] that exists only in the canvas *The Bathers*, in which the blue of the sea, in front of which the painter really does stand, is exchanged and used as the blue of the painted brook.[20] The created effect is "*[a]nother world*" of the painting, he writes.[21] There is a sense for Merleau-Ponty in which the art object itself bears a meaning-giving expressivity such that it has its own temporal and spatial aspects composing its own world. The painting's system of equivalents is a transfiguration of the represented object that confers a polysemy of meaning. An unended series of possible meanings is thus expressed in the now autonomous artwork. In the work a "world worlds" itself of its own accord.

It is by a certain misunderstanding of world, however, that the artwork's system of equivalents is seen as a mere "simulacra" in which "the order of the phenomenal is a second by reference to the objective order" or "rehabilitated as the foundation of the objective order."[22] What the painting in fact rehabilitates, what it puts on display, is not "the infra-mundane relation between objects" but a vision "engulfed [by] brute being that returns to itself," and "the *sensible* that hollows itself out."[23] For this reason *The Visible and the Invisible* refers to the work of art as a "system of equivalenc*ies*," a system in which each presented thing is interchangeable with any other possibly presented thing or series of things.[24] The work is thereby a site of differentiation conveyed from out of a "horizonal totality," but this differentiation "is not a *synthesis*."[25] A system of equivalencies here does not refer to a supra-temporal system or to an independent logic outside of time. Nor is it a synthetic act. Rather, it emerges according to the horizon of possible things that is latent only in relation to current presentations. The system of equivalencies thus addresses itself in a profound way to an otherness that grounds it, to the very logic of a sensuousness that has hollowed itself out for the sake of its apparent singularity. The point for Merleau-Ponty is that there are already possibilities in this sensible horizon that are prefigured for the artwork's own world. (It is in this connection, too, that the equivalencies in the work of art are connected to dream-work – conjuring up the anticipated.[26]) He thus also calls for an aesthetic that understands "the sense of the painting [that] is beyond the canvas."[27]

Time and again Merleau-Ponty will demand that, in order to recover the world of the work of art, we must, in fact, see how it extends beyond itself and into a palpating life of phenomenality. This may be counter-intuitive. How is it possible that the painting is both its own world and an expression of sensibility beyond the canvas? If the painting as a system of equivalencies occurs on the basis of an operant horizon, this already implicates a motivation within perception that allows for the possibility of representation. It is the horizon that grounds phenomenality, the possibility of the phenomena's appearing that determines the actuality of appearance, and informs what can be known. It is possibility that is acting upon what a conscious act intends, without making use of the belief in the real existence of an object in the order of nature. It is possibility, finally, which *motivates* the present phenomena. This exteriorization of motivation into the horizon allows us to see how things become things, to discover things emergent from out of their unifying horizon, and at the same time expressing a compulsion that is functioning in the appearing of the thing. Even if it is passively pulled into the horizon of a landscape, the painter shows that already this vision is not a subject's neutral apprehension of an object. There is, in other words, contiguity between the passivity of the painter's eye, which is drawn out into the openness of a spectatorial horizon, and the apparent impulse or motivation to represent (Merleau-Ponty will in fact use the phrase the "open circuit of desire"). What pulls the eye into its horizon, for Merleau-Ponty, is at the same time a force that bears upon and motivates the painter. This contiguity, I suggest, must itself be understood not on the basis of an inherent break between seeing and motivation but on the basis of hyper-dialectic and the process of differentiation internal to them in which they participate in an originary non-division.

There is no denying here that Merleau-Ponty understands the artwork conjointly with being. But he does so because the work of art, he thinks, never ceases to inhabit being, nor does it cease to bring that being into revelation. Being is in fact rehabilitated, then, only if we tend to the original mode of being of the work of art itself. It is through the work that we discover a being that refuses to be a foundational principle *in fact*, an otherwise unassignable moment of being's appearance. This being breaks the solidity of a semantic order to reveal a pre-conceptual relationship in and among things, a being belonging to this world rather than a different category of existence.[28] The being, discovered by artwork, dissolves the objectivity of things and their conceptual determinations, and reveals instead the moment in which it really does participate in the sensible spectacle – the secret participation of things in an unregulated harmony, a sort of cohesion underneath things without a concept.[29]

Thus Merleau-Ponty cannot *fundamentally* de-aestheticize the work of art by submitting it to a natural being. For the natural and original being that the artwork allows us to retrieve in fact prevents the work from becoming subsumed by a universal principle of explication underneath things. If the being that the artwork originally inhabits and thus recovers for us is an unregulated and concept-less foundation underneath things, this being cannot subsume the artwork into a wholly other category of existence. One should also note that it is precisely such a being that serves as the ontological possibility for phenomenology. Hence the originary character of being to which a phenomenology must return if it is truly to discover its own grounding – that is, while also remaining a phenomenology that does not posit a ground – is the very being with which the artwork is still very much intimate. It is thus with the work of art that Merleau-Ponty gains access to the radical possibilities for phenomenology. What are these possibilities?

It has already been noted that the work is a disclosing of the integral region prior to subject and object, and thus it will be equated with the process of institution that belongs to and makes possible both terms of the relation. We could say that for Merleau-Ponty the artwork conveys the inhuman depths in the human world of art. That the work of art discloses institution means, in turn, that it is not simply representational and does not simply serve to restore the original object. An image, for instance, will not literally re-present an origin. If it rehabilitates a ground, the ground it rehabilitates is the being into which a vision of specific things is more profoundly caught up. Thus the work of art signifies a deeper penetration into things without conceptualizing the being that grounds them. Here one also witnesses an art history, the periodic as well as individual styles, grounded by nonconceptual being. It follows that the work calls into question the very categories used to describe the relation between subject and object. At the deepest level, for Merleau-Ponty, the work deals neither with the given object nor with the subject to whom the object is given, neither with what is meant nor with its sense, but with their ground in being that alone has significance. This significance does not merely point into what Merleau-Ponty calls the reversibility of flesh but rather it allows the space of reversibility itself to come into the world as such. It allows us to see an inherent reversibility between the senses, or what Mikel Dufrenne in *L'oeil et l'oreille* calls a "trans-sensibility." It thus also allows us to witness a "trans-artistic" realm emergent from out of the same significance.[30]

The Relation of Art to Institution

In a September 1959 Working Note to *The Visible and the Invisible,* as well as in a passage of "Eye and Mind," Merleau-Ponty recalls Max Ernst's descriptions of the role of the painter: "to rediscover that vision of the origins, which sees itself within us, as poetry rediscovers what articulates itself within us, unbeknownst to us."[31] The painter's

role is not merely to evoke a sign for the origin of sight but to rediscover the origination of a vision laid out before the being that articulates itself in and establishes itself for that vision. The painter, in a
profound way, addresses herself to the being that grounds vision, the
being that "sees itself within us" or "articulates itself within us." To
paint, according to Merleau-Ponty, is to be responsive to this alterity,
but this response does not imply the imposition of any cognitive
operation so much as it is a dedication of oneself to the being that
grants vision.

In the very next Working Note, although with no obvious relation
to the previous Note, Merleau-Ponty describes an articulation of
being in vision as an "institution (*Urstiftung*)" that is "a sense of
transcendence . . . without any recognition of the concept."[32] A non-
conceptual transcendence is defined as "pre-empirical" or "innate."[33]
Before this transcendence is abstracted by thought, there is already a
transcendence to which one "obeys."[34] To obey, in this case, is to be
open to working from out of transcendence without taking up any
critical standpoint over the transcendence, to execute it without con-
ceiving it. Here obedience implies a transcendence that articulates its
own mode of givenness prior to thought. This submission, however,
cannot simply be to a causal or physicalistic theory of Nature that is
intelligible in itself, outside of experience. For that would imply a
Nature that, although is not itself intentional, at least with regard to
one of its proper subsets exhibits a level of intentionality (even if the
intentional level is passive here). Submission to a physicalistic Nature,
in other words, would imply what Husserl termed a common-sense
thesis, an uncritically adopted assumption that while the passive may
be true in reference to a phenomenal field, a physicalistic theory is
still true of its real ontological nature that causes the phenomenon.
But institution, Merleau-Ponty writes, is "not simply subsumption."[35]
In order to discover the passivity that truly obeys and subsists in transcendence rather than requires a subsumption by a causalistic Nature,
Merleau-Ponty refuses to let passivity just be an appearance of Nature
under specifiable conditions. Still, he recognizes, passivity by definition derives from out of something other to it. Both passivity and the
natural world to which it responds must in turn submit to something
more basic.

Here passivity is no longer intentional in the strict sense, and the natural world can no longer simply be physicalistic so much as it is that in which passivity inheres and also that to which it submits. Merleau-Ponty thus lays bare a new region of natural transcendence, understood with reference neither to subjectivity nor to objectivity, in which meaning generates itself without our explicit knowing. This discovery compensates for the difficulty described above in explaining the generation of meaning between subject and object by means of the two terms of intentionality alone. Specifically, the discovery allows us to place the relation of intentionality into what could be called a natural region of institution in order to once and for all grasp the place of the origin of meaning that happens between, and prior to, subject and object in such a way that subtends the two terms. Merleau-Ponty thus writes that institution is that which "poses itself by its own means."[36] It is "auto-regulation."[37] It thus also, and more profoundly, refers to what Merleau-Ponty describes as a "*pregnancy*" that has "a power to break forth, productivity (*praegnans futuri*), fecundity ..."[38] Institution implicates a temporality that works itself and emerges into things on its own terms. This temporality is not a coherent one, such as a realm of indissoluble and separated objectivities, but rather the inherently self-productive realm of auto-manifestation underneath and within those objectivities.

The passive obedience to institution thus serves to reveal a transcendence, prior to intentionality, out into the very pregnancy beneath things that upholds them. Merleau-Ponty thus points out a tensile structure to passivity: the transcendence discovered here, though it crosses into the pregnancy of things, also allows for a "cohesion of self with self."[39] That which articulates itself in us, and which is thus alien or unthought in us, is at the same time what coheres the self. To be a self is to be alien from oneself. It is to be held outside of oneself by something alterior, which exerts itself over the self.

Drawing out the relation between these two Working Notes it follows that, if the artwork is not derived from Nature, it originates, more fundamentally, from out of the genative principle of institution. It follows, too, that the artwork for Merleau-Ponty does not merely exhibit this genative principle of institution but also one's submission to it, that is, the way in which it has worked itself over oneself.

The question is to what extent does the artwork announce the non-conceptual transcendence of institution in such a way that it remains without a concept. The answer is perhaps a radical one: the artwork will announce the temporality of being itself into which the self transcends and to which it responds.

The work of art, Merleau-Ponty says, "rediscovers the pre-intentional present,"[40] what is called in the 1954–1955 course notes, *L'institution, La passivité* an "originary transtemporality."[41] The artwork rehabilitates a singular mode in the sequence of events, which, while it is localizable as distinct moments, nevertheless also indexes the very interiority of temporality itself. This is not to say that the work reduces events to an idea of time. It means, rather, that the work summons the temporal field of succession itself, which continually endures underneath and within localizable events. In the artwork, then, a single event proves to have either succeeded or proceeded, to have an identity as having been generated and generating, or to have an identity only within the sequencing. The artwork, for Merleau-Ponty, holds a master key to the inner gestation of things.[42] This inner gestation is a concept-less being, the retrieval of which requires a refined approach that belongs to the artist whose task, according to Merleau-Ponty, is precisely to refuse a philosophically unifying concept of things.

The work of the artist, furthermore, is to reveal the self as structured by this original transcendence and thus a passivity in relation to this transcendence. It is important to note that this is so in reference to both the subject matter of the artwork as well as in reference to the artist herself. To witness the origins of the work of art, for Merleau-Ponty, is to witness the very dismantling of precisely these distinctions. We can say here that the object appearing before the artist is not an absolute. It appears only as taking place alongside a generativity that has not yet been subsumed by thought. Likewise, we can say, the artist before whom this object appears is not a radical origin. The artist's vision always already reduces itself such that it does not merely see but, in its passivity, in fact becomes a participant in the generativity of things in general. Finally, the work of art upholds neither the subject nor the object as an absolute source of meaning. It signifies an intention emergent from out of a being that is never more than the revelatory power of a phenomenality that has given birth to both the subject and the object in service of its revelation.

The work of art signifies the vision of an artist run through with a hidden temporality in which each thing, as instituted, leads back to the logic of their institution. Things are sometimes at rest, at other times they move. Things come into being. They vanish. They are taken up or consumed by other things. Then absorbed or expelled. The ontological generativity of all this, as well as a deeply human world that transcends into it, is what the artwork according to Merleau-Ponty confers into existence. Since the artwork is in this way contemporaneous with the institution of being, the very structures of being to which Merleau-Ponty's phenomenology must return are already conveyed in the work.

We have already seen how this phenomenology conceives itself in relation not to the philosophy of art but to the work of art itself and its non-conceptual transcendence into being. We have seen that the work of art thus reveals being without appeal to a different category of existence. It will reveal the temporality of being that institutes itself in beings by means of an auto-manifestation. What more about being does this work disclose for phenomenology? The artwork, I argue in this book, will disclose an institution of being that overcomes onto-logical difference. The work will disclose an institution that usurps the difference between sense and meaning in order to announce the significance of being itself. The work will thus finally disclose an insti-tution of being in which we find things, as well as the self, to emerge from out of the selfsame or reversible space.

Institution and Ontological Difference

The work of art conveys not only things but also what discloses those things and allows us to see them. It thereby conveys an implicit response or obedience to this disclosure. Painting in its very project, according to Merleau-Ponty, thus sustains a co-genesis of the hori-zonal extension of the eye and the motivation to paint. Of concern in the work of art, for him, is not a mimesis understood simply as representation or imitation – for these are already constructions of perception that conceptually sever the thing perceived and the perception of it – but a mimetology that is related with the deep compulsion towards painterly work. Here the very notion of image is under investigation. For the compulsion to work has a direct and concrete access to the things of the horizon, which prevents the artist's vision from being extemporal and neutral. The painter's sight is in this way never merely the restoration of the origins of the work of art *en image*. It will in fact bear a physicality in which it is literally invested in things that makes it akin to touching. This tangibility within vision will be understood on the basis of an originary differentiation that allows the image to diverge or separate from out of its other.

I point out towards the end of Chapter 1, "Matisse in Slow Motion," that Merleau-Ponty's repeated references to the Paleolithic cave paintings of Lascaux are significant in the recovery of an originary differentiation. Merleau-Ponty is no different than those thinkers, such as Bataille and Blanchot, for whom Lascaux offers a site to think through the origins of the work of art. In Lascaux, after all, we discover the inscriptions of *homo faber*, who emerged roughly 500,000 years ago and who first worked with tools and was reflective about human death. The cave paintings, for Merleau-Ponty, are nothing less than a reduction to the image in its originary and natal state. This ancient image has emerged on the basis of the arbitrary features of a natural surface that has for the first time been touched for the sake of painting. The bringing-together of two foreign surfaces allows Merleau-Ponty to acknowledge the image as birthed from out of its alterior ground. The image implicitly goes out and crosses into the natural surface's plasticity or sculpturality in order to exceed the logic of vision and picture frame. It bears a spatiality and depth.

The image, in its natality, transgresses the apparently indirect and un-invested character of vision. In its archaic state, applied to the natural surface of the cave, the newly arisen image has not yet achieved the structure of representation in which there is a divide between the picture and its origin. The cave painting instead operates within a re-emancipated archaic space, which we, in fact, rediscover in vision only under the pressure of Merleau-Ponty's concrete dialectic. The space of vision, uncovered in the ancient image applied to the cave wall, implicates the alterity of a gestural space that belongs to what Merleau-Ponty calls "expression." Here, expression indicates an approach of each surface towards the other, the hand's evocation of the sensible and the sensible's pronouncements of itself in the hand. Such a gesture is not merely externally observable or measurable behaviour. Nor is it an internal or inner-directed phenomenon in which the body serves as a mere conduit of psychic impulses or of subjective intentionality. It is already a misunderstanding of expression to understand the gesture as pointing to something behind its movement or to its inner-cause, thus bypassing the gesture itself as bodily movement. The character of the movement itself is its specific quality as a gesture or as a manifestation of the artist's hand as the locus of the expression itself. This very locus of expression, we discover, indicates the alter side presenting itself in bodily expression. That is, expression requires institution. This incipient institution, we could say, defiles the notion of image. It relocates the image's origins within the convergent space between gesture and surface.

I begin the chapter "Matisse in Slow Motion" with a passage from "Indirect Language and the Voices of Silence" in which Merleau-Ponty describes the birth of Matisse's painting through the figurations of his gestures. The Matisse passage, I want to say, will at least implicitly appeal to the notion of institution in order to rectify the problem of ontological difference. The passage goes towards revealing a site of hyper-dialectics in action. It shows us that there must be an alternate grounding to both the figurations of the gesture and the surface that the gesture awakens anew. The image painted by Matisse is monstrated from out of a ground that is alterior to both the psycho-physical complex of a subject's body and the painted surface or cave as a mere object for this subject. This ground refers neither to an ideal image imagined in advance of painting nor to a logical superstructure applied in advance of the painter. Merleau-Ponty writes in "Eye and Mind" that the Matisse canvas allows us to witness the more profound "corporeal system of activity and passivity," and the figurations of the painter's gesture that is "no longer a thing or an imitation of a thing" but rather the "structural filaments" of "a pre-given spatiality."[43] Matisse says that his paintings of open windows, for instance, convey the unifying element of space, and the penetration of a horizon right into the interior of his workroom. "The boat going past the window," it seems to him, "exists in the same space as the familiar objects around . . . and the wall with the window does not create two different worlds."[44]

There is a pre-given grounding, for Merleau-Ponty, which is involved in the creative act, the surface on which this act takes place, as well as the created product. This confluence inherent to the artwork is possible since according to Merleau-Ponty the process of work from out of which the work of art emerges refers neither to the act of creation nor to the created product but to the phenomena coming forth from out of a ground in time for the sake of both. This is what Merleau-Ponty refers to in the above Working Note on institution as "flesh responding to flesh."[45] What Merleau-Ponty so famously calls the "extraordinary overlapping" of the flesh with itself (the right hand grasping the left hand) does not, as it does for Sartre, reveal the touching hand as a pure for-itself and a touched hand that is a pure in-itself. It reveals the more profound dimension of an overlap of sensations in which the hand responds to itself (the hand simultaneously touching and being touched), which is not for Merleau-Ponty just a total and violent dispute between two separate categories but rather a slippage beneath the fabric of each hand. The relation between the hands here is reversible, since the touching is touched, and the touched is touching; and this reversibility demonstrates that interiority and exteriority are manifestations of the same, at once both one's own and opened out into what it is not. This tacit non-coincidence of the hand with itself is precisely where we catch a glimpse of the fabric of being as flesh, as incarnated and subtending the hands, indeed all entities.

Flesh responding to flesh: the painter's hand is originally indistinct from a fabric of being. The singularity of the hand and its brushwork, that is, comes about not by means of its own volition and conscious activity but rather through an opening into the being that manifests itself of its own accord. Here the singularity of the artist's work allows Merleau-Ponty to introduce a notion of "style" in which the painter is opened up to what she is not. The individuated style of the painter opens into a region that is available to the other. More profoundly, this same region finally opens upon what Merleau-Ponty calls the style of being that makes mediation between the styles of various artists possible. This complex of the ways in which style articulates itself, the style of being, the style available to all subjects, as well as the style that becomes individuated, is what Merleau-Ponty in *Signs* calls "the flesh of history," referring to a being, which, as flesh, subtends the specific artistic idiom and at the same time the historico-materiality of that idiom.[46]

It may be said that, insofar as it occurs at the incarnate locus between hand and being, style is understood on the basis of a "spatial spread." Indeed, in his course notes Merleau-Ponty mentions the expression of space in Cézanne in relation to style.[47] Were it not for a spacing that crosses out ontological difference, what Merleau-Ponty calls "topological space,"[48] there could be no style. There is indeed an outside nature to spatial experience. But that this nature can be, and is in fact, presented to me implies a communion between spatial beings and the subject before whom those beings turn up. This communion for Merleau-Ponty is by no means the mark of a contradiction between two mutually exclusive and alien terms. There is an "absolute here to the there,"[49] he writes. At the same time that I find myself in a place that is indubitably mine and no other's (as in "I am here"), I also discover myself "there" (as in "my body is there"), existing and persisting among spatial beings. It is me, and only me, who is "here" but, upon reflection, I can only say this as a spatial being who is also "there." Overcoming the quotidian separation of self-consciousness and spatial experience, I find that at bottom neither can be defined separately from the other. I am opened out into the alienness of a spatiality to which I must address myself, spread out before an originary spatializing being. This is the responsivity of flesh in which, in a radical way, one finds oneself as self-consciousness only because of a spatial spread that cannot be separated from reflection.[50] At the end of a course note on creation and institution, Merleau-Ponty indicates that he is looking for sedimentation in the institution of style that does not make reference to the idea of unity.[51] Taking the definition of primal-institution from Husserl, in *The Visible and the Invisible* he refers to the sedimented as the "Earth as *Ur-Arché*" and "the carnal *Umsturz*" of this Earth.[52]

Style is a series of subversions and usurpations (*Umsturz*). It refers to the historical revolution between idioms: "To paint, to sketch," Merleau-Ponty writes in *The Visible and the Invisible*, "is not to produce something from nothing . . . this movement contains the expression with lines as well as the expression with colours, my expression as well as that of the other painters."[53] As a historical revolution, however, this does not lead to any system or esoteric logic of history. Style is instead marked by the earth-ground itself. Merleau-Ponty takes seriously the spatial spread that makes style and the unending series of subversions and usurpations between historical moments possible. Each moment is opened up before a carnal and voluminous spatiality, an operant and elemental "there" on the basis of which both subject and object are given birth. The work of art originates from out of its intimacy with an earthly surface that announces itself, differentiates itself from out of itself. The primal stroke or sweep of the painter, for instance, transgresses the mundane appearance of the thing and its outward shape in order to reach, as well as evoke, the profundity that makes the appearance possible. Merleau-Ponty writes that, in the event of creation, in "the painter's stroke – the flexuous line – or the sweep of the brush," there "is the peremptory evocation" of a "*logos* that pronounces itself silently in each sensible thing."[54]

Where the artwork is concerned, then, there is no prearranged ideality but rather the work of art is determined by a radical questioning of its own ground from out of which it has arisen in order to display that ground. The work of art, Merleau-Ponty will thus say, is "autofigurative" in that it only has its own logic as its referent. In this direct and self-intimate ability, the artwork furthermore conveys the being that, for Merleau-Ponty, is indirectly presented by quotidian things. The question is then: "[T]o what extent does this aesthetics . . . itself remain the effort of a *recuperation?*"[55] And: "To what extent does it remain 'metaphysical' in the 'totalitarian' sense: an attempt to account, as Heidegger puts it, for all beings, as such, as a whole, in terms of what is most general and what is timelessly, indifferently valued everywhere, irrespective of the differences that haunts their being as well as our accounts?"[56]

Chapter 2 of this book, "Art and Natural Being," moves more explicitly to an examination of the ground that differentiates, which characterizes Merleau-Ponty's last philosophy. A natural ontology conveys what Merleau-Ponty calls the "concrete problem of ontology":[57] it is an ontology in which he discovers the process of self-mediation between being and beings, that is, a mediation between the two terms where this mediation occurs in time and thus allows each mediated term to be unended, incomplete, unfinished, always already operant, and only understood on the basis of an inner separation or divergence from one another. Being is not totalitarian. The difference between natural being and the phenomenon does not refer to a Being which in a univocal and indifferent sense accounts for all beings. It does refer to a non-phenomenological grounding into which the rigorous investigation of the phenomenon must enter. But, qua natural being, it is not more than the *eruption of difference* between beings and their alterior side, between the visible and the invisible. Where there is individuation, then, it does not follow for Merleau-Ponty that there is an inexhaustibility of being that cannot in principle appear. It is only that we have to understand the present phenomenon as an occurrence, emergence or as a coming-into-presence from out of something that in so many ways has occurred, emerged and come forth. It is significant here that Merleau-Ponty attempts to think the flesh, in its connection to a natural being, as elemental in the Pre-Socratic sense; the elements are a "midway" or "in-between" of between being and beings. In this way being does not exceed and become more than its emergence into the present phenomenon. It is indiscriminating and *in-different* insofar as it is everywhere inhabiting beings and supplying them with a logic to their sensibility.[58]

I will say that, in its connection to elementality, being describes a notion of *physis* that is more radical than that of Heidegger's meditations, since for Heidegger there is at least some sense of a recalcitrant Being that persists apart from beings and that nevertheless grounds those beings. Merleau-Ponty's natural being, however, uncovers an incarnated principle that is the very power of emergence in the formation of entities – the internal *polemos* between the apparition of the entity and the grounding of its appearance. The work of art is precisely this struggle on display; it is the becoming of a world of entities; a site of rupture between phenomenon and natural being.

Institution and the Significant Event

It is important that both gesture and being, especially when the latter is understood as a natural being, or *physis* and elementality, are etymologically connected to pregnancy in the sense of "to birth" or "to carry." There is a mutual origination between the gesture and being that allows us to call the gesture expressive: the gesture bears a burden that cannot be alleviated merely by understanding what is behind it. The burden that belongs to the gesture is due to the fact that at the same time it emerges it also allows being to emerge or to present itself. The gesture is itself expressive because it marks a surrender to the "thereness" of its situation, spread out before an incarnate being. It is through the gesture, in other words, that the artwork is an autofiguration that brings into presence the foreign in its foreignness.

This foreignness, I argue in "Natural Being and Art," will undermine the notion that there is a formal structure to which the art object must subscribe in order to be an art object. The format of the art object is rather that of an incarnated being, which arises before the expressive gesture. Since it is the gesture that bears the burden of this otherwise alien format, making it a format only in reference to the concrete, this alienness is not pure form but already rife with content. The ontological structure of the alien within the gesture will, in fact, betray a structure of desire that is not *per se* for the thing but for the being beneath the thing, incarnating it, and thus a desire that arises not because of any free decision on the part of the artist. The artwork is in this sense the alien aspect of desire revealing itself in the process of organizing itself for the human. It is, in other words, that aspect of natural being of which the self is constitutive revealing itself as itself. This event is that from out of which things take on their specific meaning for the self, but it is prior to the categories of experience, for example the object meant and the sense of an object for a subject. The region of natural being in the self that the artwork allows to come into appearance reveals a more fundamental notion of significance. Thus the self-intimacy of the phenomenon with its own emergence and productive power to differentiate itself may be the format of the artwork, but it also displays the content of a desire that is in the act of taking shape before the human and thus the inhuman region from out of which things are significant for the human.

Chapter 3, "Proust and the Significant Event," which examines Merleau-Ponty's unique reading especially of "Swann's Way," Book One of *Remembrance of Things Past,* is in a certain sense an elaboration

of this inherent contiguousness between the horizon of the thing
and motivation. It follows, too, from the examination of the contiguousness between gesture and incarnate being as *physis*, in which we
discover the gesture's refusal to curl up into itself and its insistence to
move beyond itself into that which motivates it. This volatizes the site
of significance. It allows us to see significance in the phenomenon's
emergence and its self-intimacy and differentiating power. Tradition-
ally, we think of desire as having its own significance inasmuch as it
reaches beyond itself in a peculiar way. No action, we think, is ever
really reduced to itself since there is always a latent significance to that
action which refers to the reality of the human *in general*. The desire
for a woman, say, is never just the desire for particularity. It seeks to
grasp the subject in its entirety, to discover under some partial and
incomplete aspects of the subject the totality of his or her impulses,
his or her original relation to himself. For Proust, however, and for
Merleau-Ponty reading Proust in *L'institution, La passivité* and *The
Visible and the Invisible*, all of this is reversed.[59] Swann's love for Odette,
for instance, may indeed betray an attempt to transgress partiality
and incompleteness. But in the end, this love of the particular does
not bring Swann into any kind of totality or original relation with
himself. The sum of his impulses betrays a significant event, according to Merleau-Ponty, where the event is marked by indefiniteness
and polyvalencies. For this reason, the violinist's "little phrases" that
Swann hears one night at a dinner party are revisited by Proust time
and again: later that same evening, when Swann sees Odette for the
first time; later still, when the phrases stand in place for their love
affair. The phrases are revealed as events that have the power to forever articulate themselves anew in the present. In this connection,
Merleau-Ponty uses the phrase "the secret and patient labour of
desire" to stress that desire for Proust is contained within the site of
the original object.[60] As the site of significance for this desire, the
original object is evocative of more than just itself. It betrays a series
of relations in the sense of a world and is thus connected to the process of differentiation and the depth of being that belies this world.

 The entirety of Proust's novel is a series of images overlapping one
another, an imaginary journey from one image to another in order to

achieve the originary significant event and what Merleau-Ponty calls the labour of desire. This ceaseless layering of imagery allows Proust to reorient the codex. The text, for Proust, is plunged into image. It no longer functions as a text that seeks to render fixity to the indeterminacy and polyvalencies of the image. This relation between text and image in Proust's work is parasitic on Merleau-Ponty's critique of a language-system in the Saussurian sense in "Indirect Language and the Voices of Silence." There, Merleau-Ponty asks us to understand language not merely as its own system but in a profound sense as emergent from out of what he calls the "mute arts" and painting in particular. The notion of painting in this earlier essay is already subjected to an interrogation of its grounds in which it is shown to emerge from out of differentiation itself – a visible image arising from out of the painter's gestures, from out of tangibility and sculpturality, and finally from out of a *logos* of the sensuousness that appears for the sake of the image. Proust shows that text and the literary work of art in particular, in its profound connection to image, must therefore also be understood on the basis of differentiation. The text, that is, marks an outward deployment of an interiority. It is in this sense a space for expression, a spread in Merleau-Ponty's sense. This spread of the text allows for a space of literature, to borrow a phrase from Blanchot, in which there is an immediacy of the unidentifiable, or a showing of remoteness itself. It is this showing that grasps us, the beholders of the text, and usurps our power to grasp or appropriate it.

Institution and the Reversibility of Flesh

Chapter 4, "A Figurative Dimension: Reversibility Between the Arts," proceeds from the teachings of Proust. The literary work of art reveals the spatiality of expressivity and thus the text's reliance on the image. This image is in turn understood not merely in terms of vision but also tangibility and the figurations of the gesture. In this connection, the literary work at least implicitly makes use of a language that has not yet distanced itself from the tangible and its alternate surface. Writing (*écriture*) is in this way integral to the literary work: it makes use of the hand's inscriptions that are at the same time exscriptions, an exteriorization of the hand. This is most evident in Mallarmé's poem *Un coup de dés jamais n'abolira le hasard* (*A Throw of the Dice Will Never Abolish Chance*), I point out, which plays on the inherent plasticity and sculpturality of a poem's text. The poem, like the drawings of Lascaux, defies the logic of planarity and enframement. It is applied to any surface, even to the extent that its meaning is *determined* by the arbitrariness of the surface to which it is applied, and thus the poem, again like its Paleolithic counterpart, allows the foreignness of a spatiality and plasticity to emerge as the meaning which it intends.

The chief aim of plastic arts, I point out too, is to make explicit the latency of this spatial spread, the laboriousness of the form differentiating itself from out of its surrounding space, taking itself as its referent in order to expose its own process of emergence from within its surrounding space. The plastic arts are thus especially concerned with a chiasmic relation between the phenomenon's self-referentialism or autofigurations and its surrounding space from out of which it struggles. Rodin's sculptures, for Merleau-Ponty, present us with a movement of lines and multiple "incompossible" surfaces that depends on an inside-outside elaboration of the figure's form.[61] There is no ideal of solidity for Rodin (the same is true for the Futurist and Cubist sculptors who follow him) since the solidity, by definition, opens out into its surrounding space. This space, in turn, is interrogated by the mass since the mass is no longer a singular point or destination in space. The mass refers to its spatiality as a differentiating process that has allowed it to emerge.

This spatiality, which emerges only in relation to a being as a condition of that being, "suspends" the poem, as Mallarmé says. Such a suspense is exposed at the end of the poem's final strophe, when its last sound, as Agamben says, collapses the schism between sound and sense, between semiotic event and semantic event, or between metrical series and syntactical series. The poem is thus a directive towards the sonorous and the sonorous' relation to plasticity, the inscribing hand and the figurations of the gesture in general. Artwork is the many ways of saying difference, the space of reversibility itself that appears on its own terms as differentiation. "A Figurative Dimension" does not aim to just show the intersection between the various senses but the dimension in which the senses intersect and that artwork uncovers. It is with art, finally, through which one can think the problems that belong to Merleau-Ponty's phenomenology, beginning with institution and moving into the problems that follow institution – difference, event and reversibility.

Chapter 1

Matisse in Slow Motion

Merleau-Ponty's essay, "Indirect Language and the Voices of Silence," found in *Signs*, is a sprawling work. In it, the author has the expansive task of showing a realm of co-emergence between language, painting and history. It is sometimes remarked that the relationship, especially between language and painting, is in fact never made explicit in this essay. So underdeveloped is their convergence, it is said, that for Merleau-Ponty painting and language remain each other's equivalence, each ending where the other begins. Perhaps the most famous commentary on this relation is found in M. C. Dillon's classic book, *Merleau-Ponty's Ontology*.[1] In his attempt to clarify Merleau-Ponty's thought, Dillon first notes that Merleau-Ponty omitted several passages from the earlier version of the essay, found in *The Prose of the World*, which straightforwardly state the relation between language and painting. Merleau-Ponty writes in this earlier text that, since they are both emergent from the realm of experience that is prior to explicit expression, "everything that is true of painting is also true of language."[2] He writes again that "to signify something," means to "sublimate" the very situation to which painting exhibits a relation, and thus that signification bears a set of "roots which cannot be cut."[3] With such passages edited out of "Indirect Language and the Voices of Silence," however, this relation between language and painting is apparently surreptitiously asserted over the thesis that language is only "infra-referential" and thus without relation to anything beyond its own significative system.[4] Of course, Merleau-Ponty's task, in Dillon's words, is always to show that language implicitly contains an expressive flesh as the immanence of a whole in the parts.[5] This task entails that we see the difference between language and painting as only relative. Language might be able to "speak about it itself," but this means that it has a privileged status, that it makes a greater claim to truth, only because it sediments its primary acquisition. It cannot only be a self-sufficient system of self-referential signs, and must refer, however implicitly, to the very situation that painting reveals.[6]

Within the sprawl of "Indirect Language and the Voices of Silence," there also appears one of the most arresting passages written by Merleau-Ponty. At one point, he describes a particularly striking film of Matisse painting, and Matisse's own reaction to that film. The role of this passage may not be immediately evident to the reader, but when we look into the significance of it we see that it in fact *further* develops a solution to the underdeveloped relation between the major themes of the essay. This chapter is dedicated to establishing the relation between language, painting and history in Merleau-Ponty's thought through the lens of the Matisse passage, which I therefore present in its entirety:

A camera once recorded the work of Matisse in slow motion. The impression was prodigious, so much so that Matisse himself was moved, they say. That same brush which, seen with the naked eye, leaped from one act to another, was seen to meditate in a solemn and expanding time – in the imminence of a world's creation – to try ten possible movements, dance in front of the canvas, brush it lightly several times, crash down finally like a lightning stroke upon the one line necessary. Of course, there is something artificial in this analysis. And Matisse would be wrong if, putting his faith in the film, he believed that he really chose between all possible lines that day and, like the God of Leibniz, solved an immense problem of maximum and minimum. He was not a demiurge; he was a man. He did not have in his mind's eye all the gestures possible, and in making his choice he did not have to eliminate all but one. It is slow motion which enumerates the possibilities. Matisse, set within a man's time and vision, looked at the still open whole of his work in progress and brought his brush toward the line which called for it in order that the painting might finally be that which it was in the process of becoming. By a simple gesture he resolved the problem which in retrospect seemed to imply an infinite number of data (as the hand in the iron filings, according to Bergson, achieves in a

single stroke the arrangement which will make a place for it). Everything happened in the human world of perception and gesture;
and the camera gives us a fascinating version of the event only by
making us believe that the painter's hand operated in the physical
world where an infinity of options is possible. And yet, Matisse's
hand did hesitate. Consequently, there was a choice and the chosen
line was chosen in such a way as to observe, scattered out over the
painting, twenty conditions which were unformulated and even
informulable for any one but Matisse, since they were only defined
and imposed by the intention of executing *this painting which did
not yet exist.*[7]

Even as Merleau-Ponty omits his straightforward remarks in *Signs*,
at the same time he places the above passage on Matisse between the
first section on language and the second section on painting. It is
significant that this same Matisse passage first appeared in an essay
entitled "Science and the Experience of Expression."[8] The passage
highlights, for Merleau-Ponty, the very space of expression that he
requires after his critique of language as a system of signs. The passage, in fact, derails the significative system's claim to self-sufficiency
by showing that signs descend into something beyond themselves,
that they *mean* something beyond themselves. In "Indirect Language
and the Voices of Silence," too, this same passage has the function of
illuminating a thesis of expression in which expression is shown to
come about not on the basis of any subjective decision but rather
from out of the space that is opened up by the free movement of the
painter's handwork. Here expression is held at a distance from itself.
It is the *ek-statical* space upon which signs fundamentally depend.

Insofar as the Matisse passage allows Merleau-Ponty to show that
expression crosses over into an alterior space, and thus that expression does not originate from out of the autonomous activity of subjectivity, it also reveals that the painter's singularity is subtended by
something outside of itself. It reveals that the painter brings into
expression something that has been made available to all subjects
across the span of history. It is in the context of the transhistorical
that Merleau-Ponty takes up a dialogue with André Malraux and
specifically his works, "The Museum without Walls" and *The Voices*

of Silence. Painting, and especially contemporary painting for Malraux, discloses a subjectivity outside of history. Modern painting, he says, "frees us from the necessity of this tentative approach to the past, revealing style in its entirety – just as it displays an artist's work in its entirety."[9] The Matisse passage, although perhaps obliquely, and insofar as it shows the opening up of the gesture, reveals a common ground shared in all acts of expression. The painter's style is thus never revealed in its entirety, it is never wholly its own, since it is always opened up into an otherness that is accessible to all painters across the span of history. Style is thus what makes the historico-material idiom possible for Merleau-Ponty. It involves neither an outside interruption of a painter into the world nor is it merely a historical process that is distinct from the painter.

The themes that are central to "Indirect Language and the Voices of Silence," language, painting and history, are congeneric in the gestures of Matisse. Since the painter's gestures are the place of confluence between language, painting and history they thus reveal themselves to take place within differentiation, the logic from out of which things differ from one another, rather than point to an external logic apart from them. It is upon this differentiation, wherein the gesture is opened up into an alterior space, that a language-system is implicitly parasitic; and it is differentiation that grounds the historical without this ground referring to a transcendental logic. This is what is shown in the final section of this chapter through a consideration of Merleau-Ponty's references to the cave paintings of Lascaux. The painter's gestures ultimately refer to a prehistoric site in which we witness the origin of differentiation and it is here that we gain access to a concrete ground for style.

Language

Even the slightest philosophical reflection on language reveals a difference between what in any given case is *said* and what is *meant*. A linguistic sign might *refer*, in other words, but its referent acts only as a background that is in some sense recalled by the sign. There is a gap between the sign and the meaning to which it refers that is not

simply collapsible, and the perennial philosophical question is thus
how to understand the relationship between the sign and this background that it means. Right from Husserl's engagement with Frege,
phenomenology has reacted to the thesis that this background meaning of a linguistic sign is strictly *external* to the act of sensible perception, so that if a sign has meaning its meaning is always wholly other
to the sensible. The concept of linguistic sense may be introduced to
explain a cognitive value of relating to this meaning, but exterioriz-
ing the value of this sense in such a way that it is purely self-referential
is also problematic. On what basis does such a positing of an exterior
and independent system of linguistic senses occur?

An exterior system of linguistic senses is problematic for Husserl
not least because the notion of sense in general for him does not
refer to a self-referential exteriority, and thus a linguistic sense would
have to be understood as different in character and content from
sense in general. What he calls the noema, for instance, *is* the sense
of an act *itself* and thus it is not necessarily only conceptual, for example, the noema of an act of sensible perception. As an act of sensible
perception, the noema is a sense not at all like a linguistic sense in
which sense refers only to the appropriate sign. A noematic sense for
Husserl is not other to the sensible. It does not refer or have meaning
only through the medium of its own sense. It in fact challenges the
notion that, as a sort of timeless entity, sense by definition must
remain external to, and disconnected from, that to which it refers as
well as from the acts that grasp this referent. One can see Merleau-
Ponty's engagement with Saussure in the first section of "Indirect
Language and the Voices of Silence" in this light. Rather than positing it as belonging to its own solitary system, Merleau-Ponty seeks to
understand the linguistic sense as not more than a kind of noematic
sense. A linguistic sense, then, does not contain a background meaning that is immanent within its own sign-structure. It will not apply
only to the sign but, in its reconnection with an existential meaning,
must retain something non-conceptual beyond itself. There is, so to
speak, a non-sense within sense that ruptures its self-referentiality.
Furthermore, this non-sense of sense is by no means a background of
meaning that cannot in principle disclose itself. It is only that its disclosure will take us beyond a strict analysis of a system of linguistic signs.

But, taken on its own, Merleau-Ponty's critique of a system of linguistic signs should at least show us the need to go beyond a system.

Saussure's diachronic model of signs is described by Merleau-Ponty in different ways. In the opening sentences of "Indirect Language and the Voices of Silence" he writes, "we have learned from Saussure that signs do not signify anything and that each one of them does not so much express a meaning as mark a divergence of meaning between itself and other signs."[10] Elsewhere in the essay he tells us that, according to Saussure, "we always have to do only with sign structures whose meaning [*sens*] being nothing other than the way in which the signs behave toward one another and are distinguished from one another, cannot be set forth independently of them."[11] Meaning, according to Saussure, is referred to only by a sign and is, insofar as it is external to the sensible, immanent to the sign-structure itself. Never can we gain access to meaning *except* through the sign *itself*, therefore. Saussure thus asserts the arbitrariness of the sign, the circumstantial and contingent nature of any bond between the signifier and the signified. Words do not refer to the things themselves, as if they grow naturally from the object. They have meaning as punctuations within a linguistic structure or system. A word such as "pipe," for instance, has conceptual signification only insofar as it evokes an idea that differs from the idea of cigarette, or cigars, etc. It has syntactical signification insofar as it (noun) differs from words such as "smoke" (verb) or "smelly" (adjective) and thus cannot take their places in a proposition; and it has phonetic significations as phonemic oppositions, differing more or less from similar sounding signifiers like "pip," "pike," "peep," etc. Saussure gives to specific signs the double power of opening up and also referring to specific meanings.

We learn from Saussure that the proper analysis of language cannot be a causal one, and that a language-system is not an arrangement of natural and unmotivated facts. Language for Saussure has its own constraints and internal logic that bear upon a subject. But this demand of language on the subject, Merleau-Ponty says, remains an ideal one. It is as if for Saussure there is a "word under each thought,"[12] Merleau-Ponty writes, an "ideal text that our sentences attempt to *translate*."[13] If language operated in this ideal way, however, "the sign would be immediately obliterated by its own meaning."[14] Saussure's view alone may be untenable, according to Merleau-Ponty, since he thinks that meaning is at once both referred *to* and imbricated *in* the sign-structure. If meaning relates to language only in this ideal sense and, as such, acts as the background determining the very sign-structure that seeks to render it explicit, then so long as there are sign-structures this ideal meaning would always be disclosed with an unambiguous translucence. But this view renders the sign qua *sign* impotent, and there would be no need for it to *mean* or to *refer*. Instead there would be an eternal bind between signifier and signified.

One could say, however, that insofar as the sign does refer it points to something outside of an ideal meaning and thus it betrays a meaning not immediately grasped intellectually. Merleau-Ponty wants to show in "Indirect Language and the Voices of Silence" that Saussure's diachronic model of language is parasitic on a pre-intellectual grasping of meaning: "at the very moment language fills our mind up to the top," he writes, "it passes beyond the 'signs' toward their meaning [*sens*]."[15] Here he does not deny that the sign is intellectual but he does imply that its intellection requires mediation through a non-intellectual encounter with meaning and that this non-intellectual meaning subsumes a transcendental assignment of signifying. This implicit and mediate state indicates what Merleau-Ponty in *The Visible and the Invisible* famously calls the "paradox of expression."[16] To express something is to convert a previously grasped meaning without effacing it.[17] In "Indirect Language and the Voices of Silence," Merleau-Ponty writes that, "when one goes from the order of events to the order of expression, one does not change the world; the same circumstances which were previously submitted to now become a signifying system."[18] The point for Merleau-Ponty is that any investigation into a language system requires an investigation of this primal, sublimated state inherent to expression through which "signs take on the full value of 'signs'."[19] This requires an elucidation of "what is before expression and sustains it from behind."[20] It requires an elucidation of what Merleau-Ponty, following Heidegger, refers to as the *Vorhabe* of meaning, a pre-having, a pre-seeing and pre-grasping of meaning on the basis of which things become understandable as distinct things (*etwas als etwas*) in order for the sign to refer.[21]

Merleau-Ponty does borrow Saussure's notion of "phonemic oppositions," but he does so in order to discover what sustains expression.[22] Phonemic oppositions, in other words, allow Merleau-Ponty to address the difficulty of origination in the relation between signifier and signified. The notion that the sign originates out of phonemic oppositions indicates that it is not just an utterance, and that the sign is therefore a vocal matter, but that it is gestural and that it thus surpasses itself toward a sense that always presents as significant. A complete theory of the sign must disclose this non-ideal or non-conceptual aspect of the sign. It must shed light on the archaic relation between what Merleau-Ponty, referring to a probably Stoic distinction, calls the *logos endiathetos* (the word conceived) and *logos prophorikos* (the word uttered, the motility of speaking).[23] In fact, it must disclose the primacy of the latter *logos*. A primacy of the mouth, the tongue, breath, the lungs, etc., reveals that words are at bottom practical. "[T]he speaking subject," Merleau-Ponty says in another response to Saussure in *The Visible and the Invisible*, is the "subject of *praxis*" who "does not hold before itself the words said and understood as objects of thought or ideates," but rather "betakes itself unto that place."[24] The praxis of speech reveals a linguistic structure of transcendence. It is a doing that can hardly be described as a content of consciousness (bearing in mind the phenomenological meaning of *Inhalt*). It is a doing, rather, that happens between humans or between the human and the non-human world. The praxis of speech thus reveals what Merleau-Ponty calls "the animal of words."[25]

Speech reveals a lateral openness into the world that prevents language from becoming a system of pure significations. Language is always derivative of a concrete fact. The subject who speaks does not stand outside the development of language. Meaning is explicated, exhibited and explored through speech. It is in speaking, finally, in the precise moment that language reveals that it is primarily living, that the subject betrays an ontological dimension that corresponds to an originary event of language. When she opens her mouth to speak her words are words to be heard; they occur on the basis of a sonority inherent to the practical, where this sonorous quality reveals the sign as insufficient in itself. It passes beyond itself, into a silence not belonging to any one sign but rather grounds the sign. There is an *ek-stasis* of signs, what Merleau-Ponty calls the "silent transcendence" of language or the "the background of silence which precedes it . . . without which it would say nothing."[26] Thus, for Merleau-Ponty, there can be "no absolutely transparent signification."[27] It is not a non sequitur from the silence of language to the gestures of painting when Merleau-Ponty says that "hidden in the empirical language," by which he means the explicit sign-structures, "there is a second-order language in which signs once again lead to the vague life of colours."[28] What is at stake in painting for Merleau-Ponty is nothing short of the thesis of expression that ruptures the eternal bind between signifier and signified.

Painting

If Merleau-Ponty asserts the dependency of language on this vague life of colours, which painting puts on exhibit, and thus also questions the apparent autonomy of linguistic sign-structures, he does so even against the claims of certain painters. Magritte's eponymous painting *Ceci c'est n'est pas une pipe* in particular may be seen as an unending play on the incommensurability between language and vision, between seeing and saying. In painting the familiar object of a pipe in a very literal style, making the pipe unmistakable, and writing underneath the image "this is not a pipe," Magritte highlights the idea that the name of the thing is "really an artifice."[29] It "merely gives us a finger to point with," so that we might "pass surreptitiously from the space where one speaks to the space where one looks."[30] The image and word, the figure and text, the drawing and legend, are no longer bound by resemblance for the painter. He wants to paint the essential difference between language and things. It is not enough for Magritte to say that there is a gap or space between the two regions. Between words and things there is rather a total effacement of commonality between the signs of writing and the lines of the image.[31]

We have not as yet seen Merleau-Ponty giving an adequate response to a challenge such as this. Thus far the diachronic model of signs apparently only runs *parallel* to Merleau-Ponty's own thesis of expression, even if the former is supposed to be parasitic on the latter.

The apparent difficulties with Saussure's diachronic thesis are not arguments *for* Merleau-Ponty's own thesis of expression. Merleau-Ponty needs not only to problematize the notion that linguistic signs are arbitrary in the narrow sense that they do not refer to any thing, not only to show the need for a thesis of expression in which what is meant inheres in existence, he also needs show that the divergence between the sign-structure and its meaning does not lead to a *conceptual* significance. There is meaning to our linguistic sign-structures for Merleau-Ponty only inasmuch as this meaning is previously grasped non-intellectually and in motility.

I want to say that the passage on Matisse, intervening between the first section on linguistic signs and the second section on painting, in fact makes plausible Merleau-Ponty's claims about signs. Through Matisse, in other words, we are able to see the implicit mute realm of consciousness, the realm prior to explicit expression, upon which Merleau-Ponty's theory of signs relies. The Matisse passage, I want to say, reveals the primacy of the *logos endiathetos* in sign-structures. The passage reveals that *ek-statical* spacing or distancing that is prior to linguistic signs in order to destabilize a language system by taking away the sole power of the sign to be imbricated with the very meaning to which it refers. The following reflection on the Matisse passage reveals the distance upon which a system of signs is parasitic.

The Matisse passage first tells us why we cannot think of the painter "like the God of Leibniz," why it is not as if Matisse's painting, filmed in slow motion, elaborates the painting of a preconceived figure. To paint is not simply to paint what is necessary, not simply to discover the single brushstroke that, unlike the others, is essential. It might well be that conscious activity operates in Matisse's painterly gestures. But were the artist to enslave himself wholly to the authority of technical procedures, he would find it impossible to paint. Activity is liberated precisely when the artist is willing that his hand should move freely, allowing the result to be unpredictable. In each improvised stroke, Matisse opens up a new framework within which creative forces can be said to have free play. Indeed, for Merleau-Ponty the painting is a *happening*. The "work is in progress," and it is "in the process of becoming," he writes. Matisse's first gesture extends into a "still open whole" at the same instant it configures for each following gesture an "arrangement which will make a place for it." One might say that Matisse's successive gestures thus occur in a space of conflict, for each brushstroke deviates from the previous one and at the same time deforms another possible stroke that was not previously possible. A viewer of the slow-motion film may be led to believe that Matisse's painting occurs in a "physical world where an infinity of options is possible." But, in fact, it happens in the physical world of conflagration, in which the strife between heterogeneous possibilities is not settled by one principle or fundamental order. An aesthetic choice does not come after a survey of "all possible lines," in other words, it emerges within "the world of perception and gesture" in which, if there is hesitation, it is because of the hand's free play.

Matisse is guided by a painting that "does not yet exist" only when he begins painting, not before. The painting that is not-yet is thus emergent on the basis of a gesture that never has before it an ideal painting. The painting to come, we might say, morphs in accordance with the hand, creating and cancelling out the unformulated conditions that arise with each stroke. The at least implicit connection here between the physical world of conflagration and the free play of the painter's hand brings into focus an imaginary space, in a literal sense. I am referring here to the imagination in its many usages – *yester, phantasia, eikasia, imaginatio, Einbildungskraft, fantasy*, etc. – all of which characterize, in different ways, an ability to convey the absent in the present or the possible in the actual. For Merleau-Ponty imagination thus stands for the functioning of an un-conscious of consciousness, which is homologous with the painter's hand and gesture. It is Matisse's gesturing, after all, that opens up for him the imaginary space of a hitherto "unformulable" painting. In this sense, the painter stands at a distance from himself; his hand, advancing into the void of a "still open whole of his work in progress," also opens up this void. His gestures occur within a separation, and they are an act of this separation. In gesturing, we might say, Matisse is anterior to himself even before he is a self.

It is important for Merleau-Ponty that Matisse's own being as a gesturing-body is precisely what escapes the painter, not only through the hindsight of film but also in the becoming of the artwork. For it is these processes of escape that constitute Matisse as un-conscious.

Merleau-Ponty's passage thus calls to mind an important problem: If the painterly gesture operates by articulating the imagination and allows what was previously hidden to show itself, it could be said that the artwork reconciles the two principles of pleasure and reality – it arranges an un-conscious and confers existence to what has hitherto never been. It may be pointed out that on the basis of a convergence between these two principles, Merleau-Ponty also reverses what Mallarmé famously called the *parole brute* and the *parole essentielle*. For Merleau-Ponty what is essential and what is meant in language is the background of an un-conscious to consciousness. But this background is what one uncovers in the arrangements of the gesture. Here Merleau-Ponty can be said to re-emancipate the primacy of the *logos endiathetos* in language. What we ordinarily think of as irremediably servile, the unexceptional, banal body that is an instrument entirely subject to ends outside itself, is in fact the very background of language that sign-structures mean. The meaning to which a sign-structure refers is not opened up by that sign-structure so much as by the new arrangements that emerge from out of the painterly gesture.

One could say that in "Indirect Language and the Voices of Silence" the gesture is precisely the place of estrangement on which Merleau-Ponty's thesis of expression relies. In the last few sentences of "Science and the Experience of Expression," Merleau-Ponty suggests that we need to "perform a reduction on language," in order to be taken "back to what it signifies."[32] We need to see language, he says again, against its original background of the "other acts of expression which do not have recourse to language," to see "language as one of these mute acts."[33] To see these silent forms of expression in their relation to language is to bear witness to an emergent meaning, distant from sign-structures and yet within them. When placed in "Indirect Language and the Voices of Silence," the Matisse passage allows us to perform this reduction and to see the painterly gesture as occurring within that space between sign and meaning. The passage thus shows us what might be called the "incorporeality of sense," a "body saturated with signification."[34] The following passage, which Merleau-Ponty originally presents analogically, should thus no longer be understood as such: "language is expressive as much through what is *between* the words as through the words themselves, and through what it does not say as much as what it says; just as the painter paints as much by what he traces, by the blanks he leaves, or by the brush marks he does not make."[35] A reduction on language, seeing language in the context of painting, shows the traced line and the not-traced line as ingredient within language. The silent realm of the painterly work *is* the expressive space between words as well as in what is not-said, and that Matisse's gestures *are* "the silent background of language, the threads of silence that language is mixed with."[36]

History

History intersects with art, and thus with the fact of creation. There are two dominant trends in the historical analyses of such an intersection that immediately come to one's mind: there is the trend that is above all sensitive to the uniqueness of the work, the trend endorsed by Malraux; and there is the trend that above all concerns itself with a superstructure that binds works in order to see how each unique work comes about through an impersonal history, the trend of course endorsed by Hegel.

The former trend in historical analyses concerns itself with the origin of the work of art, a theory of production rather than of the product. What we gather in such a study is a style of the artist that is understood purely as a singular expression of the creator. The relationship between painters in this case is a history of discontinuous events. One cannot speak of an objective significance in painting here but rather the way in which El Greco, for example, responds to a direct challenge addressed to him by Tintoretto. This direct challenge offered by one painter to another is a challenge that resists history. It is a challenge that exists, as Malraux says, only in a "museum without walls." It is as though for Malraux the paintings hung on the walls of a museum show us an art-history that is profoundly ignorant of the challenge issued between painters, the challenge from out of which a style emerges and is thus essential for the painting to be. But painting, and modern painting in particular, in explicitly freeing itself from traditional forms, lacks the tentativity of the historical bind of the museum's walls. Modern painting, for Malraux, understands style as that which falls outside history and seeks to reveal itself as an excess. As he says in *The Voices of Silence*, it "gives us our bearings in our rediscovery of art's 'sacred river' by setting up painting as something that exists in its own right."[37] In "Indirect Language and the Voices of Silence," it is precisely this view against which Merleau-Ponty is working. It is true for Merleau-Ponty as well that the museum is indifferent to the inner-nature of painting– "it kills the vehemence of painting," and is "the history of death," he writes.[38] Yet for Merleau-Ponty there is no style that is purely from out of a discontinuity and thus that can be "revealed in its entirety," as Malraux put it.

But neither does Merleau-Ponty want to say that the painter's style betrays what he calls the "official and pompous history."[39] There is no essentially anonymous historical process for Merleau-Ponty, no historical relation between painters that is determined by some external superstructure. For such a history requires us to "speak of a Reason in history or of Super-artists who guide artists,"[40] which, "makes the painters as mysterious for us as octopi or lobsters."[41] The Hegelian view of art-history, in other words, empties particulars "of their finiteness and power of impact," and thus "embalms"[42] them by raising them to level of "the Spirit of Painting."[43] Merleau-Ponty takes this Spirit of Painting as presenting us with the problem of causation: the historical process exists externally to the very individuals that it is said to cause, and thus the individual may be said to punctuate or interrupt Spirit. In this sense, a Spirit of Painting resists the inner-life of the painterly work and is "external to itself," "appear[s] only in the museum."[44] "Hegel is the museum," writes Merleau-Ponty.

He also writes that the "Hegelian monstrosity is the antithesis and complement of Malraux's individualism."[45] The opposition between the so-called museum of history and the individual threatens to remain forever, and this threat is contained in their already rarified approach to philosophy. The thought of each, we may say, is the principle of non-contradiction put into application.[46] Either there is the impersonality of an art-history or there is the supreme personality of the painter. Each gives the schema of a pure vision with which the philosopher coincides, Merleau-Ponty says, and neither philosophy can admit its other into the same. But this pure vision implies, too, that both the thought of history and subjectivity raise an abstracted principle of non-contradiction over and above lived-experience, and in each case "the thought, precisely as thought, can no longer flatter itself that it conveys all the lived experience."[47] To both the structure of history and the structure of subjectivity, then, the original density and weight of the lived-experience remains a mystery, and this is what phenomenology generally seeks to resolve. In its return to experience, it aims to render the experience that is intelligible in its own mode of being. Phenomenology does not move towards a thing that is said to *stimulate* or *cause* my perception in order to understand my experience of it nor does it seek support from some principled foundation. The inner-life of experience is what phenomenology wants, and Merleau-Ponty's critique of both Malraux and Hegel is not more than a phenomenologist's critique.

In returning the principles of thought to the lived-experience from which they originally arose, in restoring the density and weight of lived-experience within philosophy, phenomenology can no longer understand the for-itself of an artistic moment with Hegel, as "an organism" caused by the in-itself of "an inherently articulated totality."[48] An artistic idiom, for Merlreau-Ponty, cannot swallow up its entire past by being an instantiation of a totality that, as Hegel says, gives "the grace of animation."[49] Merleau-Ponty asserts his thesis of art-history as against the Hegelian view in the following way:

> Painting fulfills a vow of the past. It has the power to act in the name of the past, but it contains the past as a memory for us and not in its manifest state. Even if we know the history of painting too, the past which is present in a painting is not memory "for itself" – it does not pretend to sum up what has made it possible.[50]

Here the history of art is understood as an unfolding happening within the present idiom, so that, without it implicitly indicating a view towards some animating totality, the idiom can be understood as only gaining a certain perspective on a process that innerly upholds it. One might also see here that Merleau-Ponty's notion of art-history only dispenses with a dialectics understood on the basis of causation or an instantiation of a logic external to it, and that it does not in fact dispense with dialectics *as such*. At work in Merleau-Ponty's notion of art-history is what he calls in *The Visible and the Invisible* the "hyperdialectic." This "good dialectic" returns to the most ancient sense of *dialegein,* which means to welcome difference.[51] It consists not in the erection of an external logic that mediates two terms and binds them but rather in being open to the very process of differentiation itself, as it arises in the phenomenon itself, in order to bear witness to the concrete origination of truth. Here the "for-itself," for Merleau-Ponty, must be understood as presence to differentiation and the locus where difference manifests itself. It thus discovers itself as not more than "the culmination of the separation (*écart*) in *differentiation.*"[52] The rediscovery of this good dialectic is at work when Merleau-Ponty says in "Indirect Language and the Voices of Silence" that, "the style of each painter throbbed in his life like his heartbeat." Style, he continues, is a "living historicity," a "secret, modest, non-deliberated, involuntary" life in which a painter, "recognize[s] every effort which differed from his own."[53]

Style, then, implicates for Merleau-Ponty a deep involvement in the very location of differentiation itself. Neither is style a pure identity nor is it a pure difference. Style implies neither that the painter is pure particularity nor that difference is external to the painter. It crosses out both the ontological difference and the different systems of significations articulated by a logic of history. It is the very birthplace of the distinction between the painter's own style and a historical procession. Style is in this sense *contemporaneous* with differentiation. It uncovers a being-within the ontological dimension of differentiation. It requires a stepping beyond oneself, a dwelling in things different from oneself. At the same time, style is also a coming back to or grasping oneself *through* those things. A particular style's interpretation of the past, present and even future is in this way a retrieving, recuperating or reorganizing of the implicit difference available to a painter. It is thus possible, according to Merleau-Ponty, to uncover in the articulated style a hidden "history of painting, which runs from one work to another" on the basis of "the caryatid of our efforts, which converge by the sole fact that they are efforts to express."[54]

One can speak here of a more basic "flesh of history" that avoids both Hegel's Spirit (there is a movement between painters that is not superstructural), as well as Malraux' super-individualism (there is individuation that is not a-historical).[55] There is for Merleau-Ponty a unification underneath the history of painting but only in the sense that the singular gesture of pictorial expression also secretly refers to every other across history by virtue of a communality in their origination. The origin of style is still a universal sensible in the sense that it takes hold of all bodies and binds them together. The painterly work comes to be on the basis of an appearance that does not appear from within itself but from a common ground shared by all appearances. But it is important to see that this commonality for Merleau-Ponty escapes the visibility of representational consciousness. It is a commonality that is always incomplete, a unity brought about by differentiation itself. This differentiation is located within, and not supervenient to, the particular style; and each style must address itself to an otherness always already penetrating it from the inside.

Style thus implies a particular effort or expression on the basis of differentiation, a particular historical moment as being initiated by the process of difference that runs underneath and within it. In order to grasp this differentiation as the basis for the history of art, "Indirect Language and the Voices of Silence" pays close attention to the Husserlian word, "*Stiftung* – foundation or establishment – to designate first of all the unlimited fecundity of each present, which precisely because it is singular and passes, can never stop having been and thus being universally."[56] In *The Visible and the Invisible*, too, Merleau-Ponty writes of the Husserlian notion, *Stifung*:

> It is the fundamental structure of *Zeitigung*: *Urstiftung* of a point in time . . . this latent intentionality, intentionality ceases to be what it is in Kant: *pure actualism*, ceases to be a property of consciousness, of its "attitudes" and of its acts, to become *intentional life* – It becomes the thread that binds, for example, my present to my past in its temporal place, such as it was (and not such as I reconquer it by an *act* of evocation) . . . the possibility of this *act* rests on the primordial structure of retention as an interlocking of the pasts . . . [57]

Merleau-Ponty also refers to the "*Stiftung* of a field or an idea" and "the installation in a space."[58] He describes *Urstiftung* as a "restoration of life without *Erlebnisse*," a "monumental life."[59] Finally, he speaks in another Working Note of the "the simultaneous *Urstiftung* of time and space that makes there be an historical landscape and a quasi-geographical inscription of history. Fundamental problem: sedimentation and reactivation."[60] In this last instance, we also see that for Merleau-Ponty the notion of *Urstiftung* is connected to a landscape or geography that allows one to be historically inscribed. In that same Working Note, then, Merleau-Ponty also writes of the "Earth as *Ur-Arché*" that "brings to light the carnal *Urhistorie* (Husserl – *Umsturz*)."[61]

Merleau-Ponty, paying close attention to Husserl's 1934 "Ursprung" essay here, notes that the Husserlian life-world requires an openness in two modalities, an openness to the world-as-horizon and to the earth-as-ground. Husserl is led to assert a world-horizon that is not itself susceptible to becoming the object of perception but which acts as the constantly present backdrop to our sensorial experience. This horizon first requires an earth that does not resist our sensorial efforts but rather sustains them. This earth-ground is a pure depth of supporting solidity and repose, a property without substrate, a content without form, which sustains everywhere the spread of a spectacle extended along spatial axes before the upright stance of the human.

It should be noted that these two modes of the life-world, "do not acquit [Husserl] of posing the historical constitutional questions concerning not only how we got there, but what history we are bearing, what time of directionality, what gait in our walk, what modes of spatiality and temporality we have in relation to which all other things will have sense."[62] These two modes of the life-world are in fact formative of what he calls "territory." Territory names "the generation of meaning being constituted as being reproduced through the generations (no matter how familiar or remote these past generations are) in narrative, myth, ritual, practical activities, historical events . . . "[63] Territory is the horizon of generational history that in part makes up a world that emerges on the basis of the sustenance of earth. Territory, in other words, does not operate on the background of an historical principle. There is, rather, a concrete and incarnational background of earth to generativity (change in generations). We could say: the brute, contingent fact of birth and death are the conditions of possibility for the constitution of an objective and historical world.

One can speak of style in the context of this territory in which an historical world emerges from out of an earth that grounds this world. In each brushstroke there is literally an inscription of historical events in one's practical activities, a way of being that is always already delimited as an individual's historical, cultural territory and normative significance. This particularity exemplified in the brushwork, for Merleau-Ponty, comes about from the ground of a sheer earthly carnality, which sustains the work. Impressionist technique, for instance – loose brushstrokes that dispense with "ideal contours," and instead uses 18 colours without a break up of tone in order to achieve shapes with no gaps between them or delineated edges – exhibits a particular way of being that both differs from and prepares the way for the bold colours, distorted forms-in-dissolution, and two-dimensional a-perspectival expressionist technique. While Merleau-Ponty is interested in explaining how such technical procedures come to be in relation to one another, the emergence of Expressionism from Impressionism can appeal neither to a causalistic superstructure nor to the discontinuity of individuals for whom influence is only an *ex tempo* possibility. For Merleau-Ponty, the differentiation that happens between the brushwork, colouration and technical procedures of painters is instead the effort to express on the basis of a carnal and earthly ground that sustains painterly working. There is, in other words, a carnal *Urhistorie* spread out on the basis of an earth that is the *Ur-Arché*.

One might wish to treat Merleau-Ponty's notion of style as emphasizing the carnal process – the flesh of history – that sustains historical inscriptions over an investigation into those very inscriptions themselves in such a way that carnality erases history proper. This view is given support if we understand Merleau-Ponty's move towards a philosophy of institution as a turn away from his philosophy of expression. R. Vallier argues in "Institution: The Significance of Merleau-Ponty's 1954 Lectures at the *Collège de France*," for instance, that the notion of institution eventually "has capital importance for Merleau-Ponty and for every aspect of his work"[64] because institution,

> functions independently of the subject in the perceived world, and is
> able to take account of continuous recreation and the ontological

anteriority on which it depends in a manner that expression cannot precisely because expression ultimately remains prisoner of a philosophy of consciousness.[65]

Vallier wants to say that any philosophy of expression inevitably remains within the trappings of objective thought because it is forced to rely on or offer remedies to the subjectivity that is inherent in constituting consciousness. Not even the gesture of expression seems to avoid this problem of constitution. For instance, "the difficulty" in Merleau-Ponty's thought, writes Lyotard in *Discours, Figure*, is that

> the gesture is relative if not to a subject, at least to a kind of subjectivity, be it an anonymous one, or be it nature, as Mikel Dufrenne says. It is experienced, lived or in any event it structures the lived; it is based upon . . . the subject of constitution.[66]

Merleau-Ponty's analysis of an expression in the gesture, according to Lyotard, does not undermine the subjectivity that it tries to destabilize. However much Merleau-Ponty is at pains to show a gesture pregnant with the otherness from out which it emerges, still it seems that, qua *expression*, it must constitute and, in constituting, it cannot remove itself of activity and objectivity. On this view of expression, Merleau-Ponty would need to turn to a notion of institution in order to overcome these apparent shortcomings. But such a turn, understood as distinctly different from a philosophy of expression, either prevents a discussion of the polyvalencies of a historico-materialism, or else a historico-materialism would be in the service of ontology in such a way that it ceases to be what it is.

There is no real departure from expression in Merleau-Ponty's thought. A philosophy of institution does not usurp expression. It is true that as soon as there is expression for Merleau-Ponty there is another world, which is the world of explicit meaning. But a philosophy of expression is of value for him only if it can be seen to create space for an alienness into which it opens. It is not then a matter of *deriving* an order of institution from expression. It is a matter of grasping and recovering, from within expression, its foundation. This archeological movement in fact requires an interrogation of expression in order to uncover an expressivity no longer coupled with the world but lost outside in it.[67] It is, as Merleau-Ponty says, the movement and motility implicit to expression, for instance, which finally returns expression to a pre-meaningful source in being.[68] (There are territorial expressions only because there is a ground upon which they occur).

It must be noted in this connection, furthermore, that in *The Visible and the Invisible* the rediscovered ontological source of expression is spoken of in terms of an inner-incongruence or a "paradox of being."[69] This being is not the other world of classical ontology, for Merleau-Ponty. Rather, the ontological paradox lies in that it is recuperated by what is only apparently other to it. The paradox lies in that it is found in a deep investigation into expression, discovered only indirectly, as Merleau-Ponty says.[70] We really do dis-cover institution, in turn, not by abandoning expression but by seeing that expression penetrates beyond the exterior aspect of things in order to announce their "internal movement" and their "secret ciphers." It is especially in the painter's expression, for Merleau-Ponty, that we bring into focus "the things themselves from the depths of their silence, to expression."[71]

In short, the paradox of being requires the paradox of expression. This mutual reinforcement between the paradoxes is already suggested in "Indirect Language and the Voices of Silence" when Merleau-Ponty refers to expression as the "accomplishment and brotherhood" of *Stiftung*.[72] In its inner-fraternity with being, expression is a "metamorphosis" in the sense of "a response to what the world, the past, and the completed works demanded."[73] Expression is no doubt destabilized. It extends beyond itself, and goes out into the institution of being to which it is a response. This being on the other hand demands specificity – it *institutes* difference. It requires expressing, to be taken up and sublimated. This is what style does for Merleau-Ponty – it is the paradox of expression taken to its extreme, bringing to light a process of *differentiation* without yet being *different*. In other words, for Merleau-Ponty the notion of style implies a considerable enlargement of expression such that it is no longer merely a human possession but also belongs to the inner-processes of being. The painter's style is the locus of this mutual enfranchisement. In the very same passage,

Merleau-Ponty can thus use the doublespeak of a "gesture of expression," a body that is "already *primordial expression*," which at once also "inaugurates an order and founds an institution or a tradition."[74] The gesture of expression *partakes* within the inauguration of differentiations in order to allow a new tradition to then be instituted.

The apparent contemporaneity between the singularity of a painter's gesture and the being that institutes it forces us to wonder about how there is an originary weight or priority in the relation between the gesture's expression and the being that institutes it. Merleau-Ponty himself raises such a question in the following way:

> the gesture of expression, which undertakes through expression to delineate what it intends and makes it appear "outside," retrieves the world. But already with our first oriented gesture, *someone's* infinite relationships to his situation had invaded our mediocre planet and opened an inexhaustible field to our behaviour.[75]

Here Merleau-Ponty appears to go beyond the last few sentences of the Matisse passage since here he outlines the possibility of grounding the gesture. In the Matisse passage, on the other hand, he only goes so far to say that there is for Matisse, "twenty conditions which were unformulated and even informulable for anyone but Matisse, since they were only defined and imposed by the intention of executing *this painting which did not yet exist.*" There is *no* unformulated and informulable condition, *no* painting that did not yet exist, *until* there is Matisse's gesture of expression. But each brushstroke made and painting formed, and even the unformulated conditions and paintings that are not-yet, are upheld by a mediocre planet into which the actual strokes and possible paintings must not only penetrate but also recuperate.

In what sense, then, is the gesture of expression, opened up by Matisse himself, also occasion to retrieve an ongoing process of differentiation from within the backdrop of this mediocre planet? Let us imagine what Jean-Luc Nancy in "Painting in the Grotto" calls the "unimaginable,"[76] the moment just prior to the painter's inaugural gesture. At this point neither has the gesture arranged for itself an imaginary space, nor has it yet inaugurated or instituted a "new tradition."

Since Matisse is not "the God of Liebniz" who has before him an ideal picture, unlike its subsequent gestures this filial gesture has no predecessor to follow. In fact, prior to this initial and naïve gesture, this first oriented gesture, there is *not even the painter for whom* an infinite series of possible relationships exists. Such a gesture cannot be merely motivated by the painter, then. It cannot give birth to itself. It extends into the void that precedes it, but this commencement is at once also an allurement. This simultaneity thus announces an alienness within expression coming into presence, an appearing of being that is the unsuspected reverse side of presence. Here the imaginary space of the painterly gesture, reclaiming the neutralized "image," is no longer "thoughtlessly believed" to be "a tracing, a copy, a second thing."[77] It rather exposes a "duplicity of feeling [*le sentir*]," that is due to "quasi-presence and the imminent visibility which make up the whole problem of the imaginary."[78] The gesture that arranges an imaginary space, in other words, is subtended by an "unimaginable" institution, the very process that differentiates it. It is invested and wandering out into that process. This is mimetic in the truest of senses: the gesture of expression really does mime the monstration of being; it is a silent gesture playing at the outlines of the very formation of invisibility.

Matter or Style?

Merleau-Ponty's formulation of the image as a quasi-presence and immanent visibility is, in the first instance, a rejection of the metaphysical aspects of aesthetics, which posits a dichotomy between copy or image and the origin, aligning the origin with the realm of Spirit while relegating the image to the realm of sensuous matter. The gesture shows for Merleau-Ponty that, in the event of creation, both the origin and image are simultaneously engaged, and thus that the origin of the artwork is not to be separated from the created product nor is this product merely a double of its origin. The gesture, that is, diffuses the metaphysical distance between Spirit and sensuous. The gesture that is connected to the Latin root *gerere*, and thus "bears" or "carries" a sensuousness, is the same gesture that Merleau-Ponty says in "Eye and Mind" is "birthed" by being.[79] Gesture is of course typically associated with movements of the hand, and the hand especially, Merleau-Ponty says, carries being into expression at the same time that it is ignited and gestated by that being.[80] The primacy of the gesture in aesthetics brings the realm of art back towards an earth that functions as the point of origination from out of which the various arrangements of the gesture arise. In order to recover the origins of the work of art, Merleau-Ponty has to show how this earth grounds both the image and the gesture that carries that image into expression in such a way that they each reduce back into the earth. Merleau-Ponty has thus sought to show that the earth, following the Husserlian formulation, is a field-structure that institutes both gesture and image and is thus sedimented in both terms. This sedimented carnality, for Merleau-Ponty, institutes itself at any time and sustains any possible painterly effort. It is a carnal *Urhistorie* that binds each epochal style. This commonality within each style is, furthermore, not a singular point of origin but the differentiation that allows for the coming-into-being of a world in the painterly effort.

The earth, insofar as it is the carnal ground in which differentiation occurs, is described as the *Ur-Arché* for the singular style. It is possible, however, to think of this archaic foundation of the earth as sheer materiality. In "Indirect Language and the Voices of Silence," there is mention of the Paleolithic drawings of animals in the caves of Lascaux. Merleau-Ponty also speaks of the "mediocre planet" upon which the first oriented gesture opens up an infinite series of possibilities. In this section, I want to say that if we think of the earth as matter or as extension then the role of painting in relation to its ground changes in a fundamental way. It becomes the event of a purely human construct. This view is perhaps supported by the usual understanding of the Pre-Socratic notion of *aisthēsis* as the material sense qua sensuousness that is primarily bound up in the sense of touch. The image spread across such a surface could simply partake in such a sensuousness that is there for the painter's touch yet in need of a purely active hand to spread the image onto it. But if, as I hope to show here and in the following chapter, the cave as an instance of earth-ground is not matter but rather being, then painting in relation to the cave is not a purely human construct. It rather arises from out of a specific path of being or what Merleau-Ponty will call "natural being."

Merleau-Ponty writes in "Indirect Language" in *Prose of the World*:

> The first cave paintings opened a limitless field of exploration, posited the world as something to be painted or drawn, hailed an indefinite future of painting. That is what moves us in them, makes them speak to us, and causes us to respond to them through metamorphoses in which they collaborate with us.[81]

There is a limitless field of exploration and an indefinite future for painting only after the first painting posits a world to be painted. It seems, therefore, that the history of painting must be an autonomous and entirely human endeavour. But even so there is also for Merleau-Ponty the role of the cave itself upon which this limitless field may be conveyed. It is the cave, after all, which is decorated and brought out of its previous alienness of stone, minerals, etc., and into the familiarity of the living world.

It is this transformation from alien to human world that I think is significant. There is no painterly gesture until the hand touches the cave in such a way that the cave has offered itself not as a rock but as a canvas. The cave wall, in the moment of its transformation into canvas, reveals itself as an *Ur-Arché* for the image. This moment of the cave's transformation, and the revelation that the cave functions in the appearing of the image, implies an *aisthēsis* which bears its own *logos* and which emerges or hollows itself out for the sake of an ancient gesture that touches it. The sensuousness of the stone thereby bears a depth into which the gesture extends so that that it may express this depth by rending it from its previous dissimulation. Merleau-Ponty does not understand *aisthēsis* as mere materiality, but *aisthēsis* is submitted to the depth of phenomenality and appearing and is brought back to its original meaning, the appearance of that which, of itself, shows itself. The first painterly touch upon the cave leads Merleau-Ponty back to an inner power of differentiation underneath the materiality of the stone. This power is what allows for style, for Merleau-Ponty, insofar as it opens up space between interiority and exteriority upon which style relies.

It is helpful to contrast Merleau-Ponty's use of cave paintings with Jean-Luc Nancy's in "Painting in the Grotto." For Nancy the moment in which the first painter is drawn to the wall of the cave implies an ancient gesture that rests against, and is not absorbed into, the material cave. The cave, for Nancy, is left behind in its sheer materiality. Since the painting is set against a strictly material earth, the earth retreats from the painterly work and leaves the gesture to *create* the world by transforming the rock. One notices, consequently, that there are repeated references to demiurgy in Nancy's writings on the gesture since the brushstroke is what brings about a sense of being-in-the-world.[82] In the instant the prehistoric painter touches the cave in order to paint, he says, the surface of the stone is "freed from inert thickness,"[83] transformed from a previously dead slab into a space for possible figurations, "a spacing in which to let come . . . the presence of the world."[84] Already for this primal painter, then, the sheer materiality of the cave is set back and, "[t]he world is as if cut, cut off from itself and it assumes a figure on its cutaway section."[85] There is no ontological urgency in the background of the painterly work here; for the previous inertia of the cave itself prevents any such possibility. We cannot say with Hegel that art is the sensuous expression of the Idea. For since the background of the work of art is nothing more than the material or sensuous, and since this materiality does not take the painterly gesture beyond itself and to the Idea so much as it recedes to the point of scission, then the most we can say is that the work itself contains the idea, that art is the idea and only "it forms the form."[86] "By painting the wall," Nancy thus writes, "the *animal monstrans* does not set a figure on a support; rather, he takes away the thickness of this support, he multiplies it indefinitely, and it is itself no longer supported by anything. There is no more ground, or else the ground is but the coming about of forms, the appearance of the world."[87]

There is no earth-ground, for Nancy, nor, therefore, does the world-horizon come to be on the basis of the earth acting as its primal foundation. Nancy wants to contest the very notion of a horizonal-structure in which the world arises from out of an earth.[88] The world is cut away from the cave such that the painter, for Nancy, resists seeing in terms of a horizon. The work of the artist should in fact force us to ponder how the world arises in view of its total lack of horizon. The prehistoric painterly gesture is thus already imbued with an indefinite multiplicity without reference to a universal horizon from out of which multiplicity arises. In this sense, for Nancy, the painter's world is an infinite place of dwelling *precisely because* of her finitude and singularity.[89] The infinitude of the painter's world, and its indefinite multiplicity, is brought about by the gesture that cuts away the material rock and as a result only has recourse to its own particularity and most profound sense of self-identity. This extreme moment of intimacy is enough for Nancy to question the notion of the gesture and its relation to an origin of the image apart from it. The image created by the gesture, according to him, has its own logic and radical singularity. It is self-intimate in the extreme.

Nancy says in "On Painting (and) Presence," specifically in reference to François Martin's stark white canvas, *Le Semainier*, that in the artwork "there is no scene," and that "it is entrusted to this world, its own; there is no other."[90] He goes so far as to say that *Le Semainier* forces us to question the very logic of representation:

> Colour is always the colour of "each time": each time, in each place, *local* colour, literally. This green is not that other green nor that ochre, nor that dirty blue. But this does not happen according to the differential continuity of a spectrum . . . Now there is only *this* green, *this* vermilion . . . [Martin] is the painter of a single colour: the one that repeats itself inimitable.[91]

The white of the canvas forces us to regard colours on the basis of lack rather than with the support of a darkness more general than any colour. The canvas helps us to resist seeing the particular colours of painting simply as variations of "colouration." *Le Semainier* lacks a general ground, according to Nancy, to reveal that instantiations of particular colours really carry their own meaning, animate themselves, and thus, even when they have the formal task of representing through exterior objects, landscapes, portraits, etc., function in the painting on the basis of their own intrinsic, motivating nature with respect to the objects that serves its substrata. The colour, insofar as it comes into contact only with itself, is not linked to a tonality through a set of some external and contingent associations. *Le Semainier* finally reveals, for Nancy, that colour and the form of colour are always abstract. The painting even allows him to deny that at its core colour can be spread across the thing and bind with a surface and its extension. In a certain sense, he joins Michel Henry in the latter's readings of Kandinsky. There is an auto-affectivity in each colour – a colour that is in-itself, only in relation to itself, betraying only the invisibility of its own extreme self-referentiality, and thus determined neither by artist nor by viewer.

There is no symbolism of colour for Nancy that is already unconsciously in nature. Colouration for him betrays the self-intimacy of the work of art, and is the means by which a painting gives its own world in the sense of a recurrent multiplicity without the support of a horizon. The painterly gesture, consequently, must locate the meaning of history within itself. It must betray the nuances of a dialectic that synthesizes the formal structure of meaning and real historical development of meaning. That the prehistoric gesture has already brought the transposition of a world means, for Nancy, that it always occurs within and unfolds only within itself an epochal and historico-materiality. It means, too, that the world of the work of art is already woven entirely of language, open to words and in virtue of words. Even the pictorial themes of animals in the caves of Lascaux are derived from the *fabula* of astronomy, each crude image on the cave not only depicting an astronomical formation but also the narrative that weaves itself around that formation. What defines the painting is not the silent and a-historical world of natural perception, then. The gesture can begin with a certain naivety in that it may attempt to exit its own history but it does so with full knowledge that there is a tradition not merely prior to it but *in* it, and thus the gesture, "separates at the same moment – with the same deftness, with the same drafted line – the tracing animal and his gesture: at the point of the flint or the finger springs forth the separated real . . ."[92]

Merleau-Ponty does have an argument to show why the cave wall does not recede the moment there is painting and thus why we must think of the wall as an earth-ground that differentiates. In "Eye and Mind," for instance, he points out that the cave not only lets the painting transgress the norm of a picture frame but it is also in an important sense *active* in letting the image function sculpturally. That is, for Merleau-Ponty the natural surface lets the image exceed visual representation:

> The animals painted on the walls of Lascaux are not there in the same way as are the fissures and limestone formations. Nor are they *elsewhere*. Pushed forward here, held back there, supported by the wall's mass they use so adroitly, they radiate about the wall without ever breaking their elusive moorings. I would be hard pressed to say *where* the painting is I am looking at. For I do not look at it as one looks at a thing, fixing it in its place.[93]

The image on the cave, for Merleau-Ponty, does not partake in any clearly defined pictorial space existent apart or above the rock surface – it sometimes even utilizes the rock in order to achieve more than a framed planarity – and this indicates, it would seem, an understanding of pictorial space as ontologically akin to the natural, a space beyond the simply enclosed composition.[94] (In the end, this sculpturality will, furthermore, allow us to see the meaningful background of language as that which includes the alterity of the sensuous, where this sensuousness itself includes alterity, the interpenetrability of the tangible, spatial, acoustic and visible). Rather than comporting itself to a uniquely established aesthetic vision of the world, the primary gesture does just the opposite. It never in fact breaks from the moorings of the cave's wall, and is in this sense a reduction away from the transcendentally ideal aesthetic object.

It is important to note, then, that since it is the natural surface of the cave that grounds the work of art, allowing it to overcome the enclosure of the composition, there is ultimately no exclusive foundation for art apart from things. In this respect Merleau-Ponty is uniquely situated. For the overcoming of the enclosure of the composition has in fact led other thinkers to posit a transcendental logic that belongs to the artwork alone. In *The Principles of Art History: The Problem of the Development of Style in Later Art*, Heinrich Wölfflin famously sought to retrieve what he called "*eine Naturgeschichte der Kunst*" in which we discover the facts and laws and universal forms of representation of the image. The "painterly vision" renders things not "linearly" but in "masses" in order that a viewer's attention may withdraw from the out-line to the image dominated by light and shadow "to avoid the impres-sion that this composition was invented just for this surface."[95] To lose touch with the frame, and to convey the logic of a "visual picture," implies a move, for Wölfflin, away from the "Linear (Draughtsmanly, Plastic)" to the unique and separated laws of the "Painterly Tactile and Visual Picture." [96] For Merleau-Ponty, however, since the origins of the work of art involve and put into play a natural surface there is originally no distinction between the "painterly tactile" and the "draughtsmanly, plastic." The planarity of the image achieves its openness, for Merleau-Ponty, not because of its own logic apart from things but because it is always already prolonged into an-other surface. Here the painter and the draughtsman collapse into one another. The tangible and arbitrary surface is precisely what gives the image its painterly character. The image escapes the logic of the pic-ture frame, it becomes an image, not because it represents and thus establishes itself as artwork but because what founds it as an image is tangible; and it is this tangibility that plays a part in the appearing of the image. In this sense, the surface on which the image is originally applied is, for Merleau-Ponty, an operant depth in the appearing of the image.

The origin of the work of art thus highlights a gesture that is the concrete site of differentiation. The painter's hand that touches the cave wall in order to paint does not simply touch matter. It extends beyond the natural surface, into the operant depth inherent to the material stone, in order to then come back and formulate an image. The painter's hand in this sense functions to unveil and render explicit rather than announce an entirely new pictorial world. It rends a revelatory power that functions underneath the stone, what Merleau-Ponty calls "natural being."

This natural being is not, as Nancy would have it, a "*physis* unveiled in its truth" that, because as it accentuates a "technicity," in fact "dis-lodges art from its poetic assurance."[97] The gesture that relates to nat-ural being, for Nancy, thus places emphasis on the various concoctions of paint, the tools used to make artwork, etc., all in the service of rendering the real appearance of things. But natural being, for Merleau-Ponty, denotes an unveiling that, in fact, *subsumes* technique, the technical, *technê* in the broad sense. The painter's gesture that relates to natural being, according to Merleau-Ponty, does not accentuate a technicity but, rather, it locates what he calls a style that comes into explicit appearance not on the basis of any subjective decisions but on the basis of a free play. What this free play highlights, in turn, is a gesture that does not per se "select" or "choose" between options but goes out into the world of various possible options and then confers one into existence.

In this sense, as Elkins says, the painter can make good use of the alchemist notion of the "mouldy *materia prima*," which is "not only a metaphor for the desperate impoverishment and loneliness of the first moments before creation but also a literal embodiment of them. Alchemists actually dug in swamps, and tried to brew turds and urine."[98] The work of art does not create in the abstract. It begins "*in media res*, literally in the middle of things: oil, canvas, squalor. So it is the artist's task to discern somehow what is worth saving, and what can be transformed, and finally to crawl out of the morass."[99] The hand of the painter, for Merleau-Ponty, takes place from within a morass on the basis of which options appear before it. The hand thus takes place within a natural being that subtends these options and allows them to appear before it. The artist's work is fundamentally defiled, not a revelation. This defilement is already shown in the gesture's double-use of birth with which I began this section. The gesture is birthed and gives birth. It is etymologically connected to *physis* in the sense of *natura* and *nasci*, which means both "to be born" and "to arise from." Natural being and the gesture are tightly bound in Merleau-Ponty's aesthetics. They are the mutually symbiotic supporting or chiasmic principles of the first moments of painting that allow each surface, the rock and the hand, to cross into one another.

Chapter 2

Art and Natural Being[1]

"The painter lives in fascination. The actions most proper to him – those gestures, those tracings of which he alone is capable . . . to him they seem to emanate from the things themselves, like figures emanating from the constellations."[2] The painter does not merely look upon the world. The world is grasped by the painter only through an expression that is in the thick of things. The painter's display of the thickness within expression is nothing less than an interrogation of the grounds of perception itself. It shows the implantation of the painter into the earth, the field-structure where every surface prolongs into a dimension and pure depth. What the painter thus expresses, in conveying a depth that inheres in the earth itself, is a ground that supports each surface without becoming an absolutely different category of existence from the painter. What the painter expresses, in other words, is an active principle from out of which her own expression emerges and is made possible. It was Husserl who first divined this earth-ground in his 1934 manuscript note "The Originary Ark, The Earth, Does Not Move" (to which Merleau-Ponty pays close attention). The earth, he writes there, is an "open range of possibilities," a "deformation and continual inner motion," and an "open and indeterminate horizon of earthly space."[3]

The earth, for Husserl, is not the theoretical object of a globe but rather that which sustains expression. It lacks any clear outlines or profiles, its contours are impossible to see. It resists becoming the object of perception. In fact, it cannot become the object of perception, for this earth-ground is not really space so much as it is underneath space, what sustains spatiality. Nor is it distance: "we approach it no more than we approach or quit our own body."[4] We in fact take the earth with us as we move our bodies. This kineasthetic ability becomes the formation of the earth, that is, it puts into form the otherwise informal earth, which is the realm of possible movement for the body. This realm of flow between body and earth exposes an elemental belonging-together. The presence of the earth for the body and the body for the earth is elemental in the sense that in every instance the earth sustains the body's efforts. This elemental earth-ground will allow the artwork to be brought back from abstract thinking. The delicacies of the artist's brushwork occur from out of the raw physicality of the painter's scratches, grazes, scrapings, press-ings, sweeps, dashes, strokes etc. None of these are contiguous with any-thing but depth itself, and in this sense the painting that they form is, at its heart, nothing more than a monstration of a certain inhumanity or animality of the human in an earth.

The elemental earth that sustains these efforts, I showed in the pre-vious chapter, is the dimension of differentiation between language, painting and history. For this reason, I suggest that "Indirect Language and the Voices of Silence" implicitly references a natural being. The essay is thus at some level an essay on the Greek experience of *physis* (the Greek word for nature), which names the realm of co-emergence between art, language, history etc. Natural being, Merleau-Ponty says, gives access to "the concrete problem of ontology."[5] Such an ontology is uninterested in "a philosophy of history" or in a "philosophy of man" but rather in their modes of connection – the origination of human history without the principle of universal explication.[6] How can natural being give us the principle of convergence between art, language and history without giving us a principle of universal expli-cation? Before returning to a reflection on artwork and the originary ark of the earth-ground, this question needs answering.

The first section of this chapter ("*Physis*, Nature") outlines Heidegger's analyses of *physis* and Merleau-Ponty's natural being in their attempt to overcome ontological difference. Heidegger may ultimately fail to think through the difference in his recovery of a *physis* that is always subject to the primacy of Being. For Merleau-Ponty, on the other hand, being does not exist apart from the region of convergence between language, painting and history. Such a being does not pre-side over *physis* but is synonymous with it in order to identify the abid-ing sway out of which natural event emerges as such without letting that which grounds the events stand apart from it. A natural ontology points, then, not only to the emerg*ent* physical being but also to the emerg*ing* that yields it. But this formulation of natural being is still incomplete for Merleau-Ponty: nature for him is the name for the very occurring of the originary difference of determination and non-determination, the very occurrence of an articulation of a primal difference between something and non-thing. It is both *out of* which and *within* which beings come to be.

Having thus shown that, for Merleau-Ponty, the ground of being is differentiation itself I can then continue the discussion with which I ended the last chapter: the imagery of the first painter to touch the wall of the cave. As a localization of kinaesthetic and tactile sensation it may have at first seemed that the hand is radically different than the surface it touches. But insofar as it is in fact, for Merleau-Ponty, a natural being, and thus a concrete field-structure, the cave offers itself to the hand of the painter as a kinaesthetic horizon of possible movements. Thus the hand, in a more profound sense than simply pressing against a foreign surface, mimes a logic of appearance. The hand and cave, for Merleau-Ponty, cross into one another in order to highlight a deeper place in which they first intersect and then diverge from one another. Since, as I show, such differentiation is not more than a natural being, it will follow that the origins of the work of art is natural being itself. Thus the artwork, I point out in the second section of this chapter (Nature and Art: Interrogating Formal Structure), implicitly returns itself to a ground of being in time. The artwork reveals itself to participate neither in a transcendental logic nor in a Being apart from beings but rather the incarnated and temporal principle of being. Its original mode of being, then, resists formal structure – specifically, I look at the formal elements of point, line, and colour – and refers to no principle apart from incarnation.

It is important that we remind ourselves here that the ground of the artwork, as not more than a natural field-structure from out of which difference occurs, is not *matter* in the Cartesian sense of pure extension. This matter, insofar as it is defined as that which is spatial and divisible, has the main function of submitting to a mind that stands against it. Here matter is reduced to that which is calculated and speculated about and ceases to have any power of its own to stake its claim upon the mind. But, on the other hand, when Merleau-Ponty speaks of a natural being he cannot dispense with matter altogether.

In fact, if being were unrelated to matter this would be devastating to his thought. It would be to admit that even if according to him there is a being underneath natural events these events participate in a different category of existence from being. The former would be extended but conditioned by a being that is not itself extension. This would, in turn, implicate an openness underneath natural events that cannot be converted to having, a fabric of being that is impossible to break into, or an other vis-à-vis the world because it stands against the material. This is why Merleau-Ponty also refers to being as a "worked over mass."[7] In the very final Working Note dated March 1961, he again uses the phrase "worked-over-matter – men = chiasm."[8] The material, for Merleau-Ponty, is a specific path of a movement of being. It is what he calls "a cross section upon a massive being" or a "grain or corpuscle borne by a wave of Being."[9]

The gesture that touches the cave wall to paint unveils the wall as it travels a specific path of being. The created product and its formal structure thus originates from out of a concrete logic of appearing in order to confer it into existence. The work of art, in other words, brings into existence the hitherto unexpressed unthematic and implicit meaning of things. But this unthematic meaning, insofar as it "works over mass," is not to be understood as a different category of existence. The work of art, then, begins in a region of existence that is neither the for-itself of the painter nor the in-itself of the surface that is painted. It is, in an original way, a participant in the incarnate spread between hand and cave. Thus (in Desire and Art: Interrogating Content) I want to show that, at the same time the artwork questions the notion of form on the basis that it occurs from within the spatial spread between painter and cave, it reveals for Merleau-Ponty a structure of desire that is not merely anthropogenic. This belonging-together and thus reconsideration of the terms form and content in the work of art, I want to say, allows Merleau-Ponty to say that the artwork discloses the natural being that constitutes and is prior to the self; it performs what Merleau-Ponty toward the end of *The Visible and the Invisible* describes as a "psychoanalysis of nature."[10] That is, the alienness inherent to the self, as it emerges from out of nature, makes itself apparent in the artwork.[11] The undoing of form and content in the artwork will in turn set up Merleau-Ponty's treatment of Proust in the next chapter ("Proust and the Significant Event").

Physis, Nature

Heidegger's etymological analyses show that "genesis," one of the Greek words for the meaning of *physis,* and the Roman word *natura* (from *nasci*), meaning "to be born," or "to arise from," signifies "that which lets something originate from itself."[12] But, according to Heidegger, we no longer hear the connection of nature to this coming-to-be, for by nature we understand it to mean a fixed realm, contrasted with other realms of being – a nature that is *not* art, *not* history, etc. Oddly, then, nature comes to imply for us some supernatural realm. In *Heidegger: Through Phenomenology to Thought,* Richardson points out that Heidegger may appear to re-entrench this very problem in his 1943 epilogue to the essay *What is Metaphysics?* when he writes that "Being indeed (*wohl*) comes-to-presence without beings,"[13] suggesting that, inasmuch as it requires beings, *physis* is in fact not *originally* the same as Being. But in the 1949 version of the essay's epilogue this very sentence is changed to, "Being *never . . .* comes-to-presence without beings."[14] The first statement in fact expresses the primacy of the Being-process in the emergence of beings. It indicates an ontological difference but does not yet name it *as such.* The second, 1949, statement says that, although Being must be thought for itself, to understand the ontological difference we must also understand that Being cannot *be* by itself. Thus, according to Heidegger it is possible to claim both that beings cannot be without Being and that Being cannot be without beings.[15] *This* names the ontological difference as such and, thus understood, it gives importance to a nature in which difference itself occurs, *physis.*

Physis refers to what arises from itself, what unfolds, what comes into appearance and endures in appearance. These traits are what Heidegger describes when he says that *physis* is the name for an "emerging-abiding sway," where "sway" (*Walten*) implies the movement of a force relentlessly unfolding in the form of distinctive beings.[16] A being whose way of being is *physis* thus "puts itself forth," appearing in the open, lighting up and making itself accessible to an observer. In this way, *physis* is connected to "*phuein,*" which means "to illuminate, to shine forth and to appear,"[17] and is innerly related to *phainesthai,* which is a form of *phaino* and means "to bring into the light of day." *Physis* thus expresses the idea of a "phenomenon" as defined in *Being and Time*: that which manifests itself or appears in the light, that which emerges from out of concealment in order to show forth.[18]

In this connection, *physis* undergoes the same treatment as the phenomenon in *Being and Time*, which Heidegger identifies with *ta onta*, the Greek word for beings and their beingness. "*[P]hysis*," writes Heidegger in *Vom Wesen und Begriff der Physis*, "is qualified as a mode of *ousia* (beingness),"[19] and thus to be "*physis*-blind" is "but a variety of the blind to Being."[20] Heidegger thus stresses that the Aristotelian question "*ti to on?*," "what is a being *qua* being in its Being?,"[21] is primarily an interrogation of the coming-to-presence of beings in *physis*.[22] It does not essentially ask about a Being as such, which founds beings in an ultimate and supreme ground and is neglectful of the originary apprehension of Being. Rather, the retrieval of this "being *qua* being in its being" requires us to construe a unity between thinking and being, between *logos* and *physis*. This is only seen, according to Heidegger, when *logos* is read in terms of its root meaning, *legein*. In its primary connection to *legein*, *logos* does not mean "thinking" so much as it means something like "reading-off" (*Ablese*), or selecting various items (wood, wine, etc.).[23] In assembling or gathering these specific items rather than others, differences between things become manifest.[24] And because it is originally a gathering or gatheredness of things, according to Heidegger *logos* is equivalent to the surging and prevailing presence that is designated by *physis*.

Just as *logos* lets something be seen from itself, so therefore does *physis*. Just as a return to phenomenology in the sense of a *phainomenon-logos* lets what "shows itself be seen from itself," and "show itself from itself," a return to *physis* allows us to grapple with the problem of preserving a genuine and first vision of what becomes manifest. But, again as in the *phainomenon-logos*, this return to *physis* also requires us to recognize that beings can also appear to be what they are *not*, and thus that showing can also mean what "looks like" or "seems." We must never forget, however, that this semblance is still a derivative form of self-showing, and that even in the self-showing of the *phainomenon* as something other than itself, there lies the possibility of a genuine and original access to the phenomenon. Only by giving an account of this privative character of beings, as an intrinsic way in which they could be, can we gain a genuine access to the phenomenon itself. In this way, Heidegger leads us back to *physis*, which refers to a negativity in the sense of *sterēsis* or privation at the core of a being.[25] For, since *physis* is the process by which beings and Being are unified, it shows the falsity that beings come from a negative nothing in the sense of an *Ens rationis*. What merits thought is rather the sameness between non-being and Being.

An account of *physis* and its inherently privative character also has to show that "no longer being" and "not-yet being" are fundamental and even *constituent* characteristics of natural beings. Only by showing how natural beings stand and endure, and thus presuppose a relationality among beings, all the while being subjected to this process from-out-of-which and being-toward, can we achieve the task of clarifying the meaning of the phenomenon. Clarification of a being's privative quality is of course written into the unveiling-disclosure of the *Da* of Dasein for Heidegger, its "being-the-there."[26] Being its own there, this *Da* characterizes a being-at-home in one's own place that is at the same time actualized in the threat of a nullity's immanence. The *Da* of Dasein is revealed as having a nullifying power, a locus in which the radical threat of nothing emerges. Nullity, we may say, reaches Dasein because it is *there*.

Still it is not explained wherefrom emerges this nullifying power, this lethic quality that sends nothing towards the *Da* of Dasein. In a lecture delivered at the University of Marburg in 1928, Heidegger describes the coming-to-presence of nullity as a non-negation for Dasein in the following way:

> Upon closer consideration, it turns out that even the *not* (negation), or the essence of the *not*, *nullity*, can only be interpreted on account of the essence of time, and it is only on account of this essence that the possibility of modification, for instance, of that of presence into absence, is to be understood.[27]

Differentiation is prior to modification: the modification of a being is, Heidegger wants to say, not derived merely from its coming into and going out of existence. The "no longer" and "not-yet" of a being for Dasein must rather be determined by a temporality, upon which a thing's changing occurs. This timeliness to the thing, then, cannot be understood as an essential negation of a being's modification in time. It is instead a nullity that is "lanced to the logic of the Same and the Other"[28] – that is, a nullity in the region of differentiation. What merits thought in the sameness between non-being and Being is what is coming-to-presence and the inner-process of difference itself. We are thus, finally, led to think not only of modification but also to the Heraclitean fragment 53, which famously begins "war is the father of all and the king of all." For the relation between Being and non-being is a relation in which things emerge as such and such from out of a primal strife and struggle (*polemos*) that initially draws beings out of concealment and lets them come forth as they are, having determinate characteristics in relation to each other. Seen from this standpoint, a world initially comes into being through an "originary struggle,"[29] a primordial unfolding of oppositions and distinctions on the basis of which beings come to be. This shining-forth of beings in their ways of showing up is described by Heidegger as the "originarily emergent self-upraising of the violent forces of what holds sway, the *phainesthai* as appearing in the broad sense of the epiphany of a world."[30]

The Heideggerian thesis that difference is prior to modification seems to reverse in exact measure the Husserlian notion of time-consciousness, which begins in the continual temporal modification of the primal impression. We may say that, for Merleau-Ponty, the two theses are in fact simultaneous and that there is differentiation *in* modification. There is no ontological principle of differentiation that stands apart from temporal modification. Differentiation happens in time. It is a ground that does not resist the plenitude. One grasps this simultaneity between differentiation and the plenitude in what Merleau-Ponty, in the "Interrogation and Dialectic" chapter of *The Visible and the Invisible*, calls the a "philosophy of interrogation." To interrogate the self-sufficiency of the plenitude is to discover a nega-tivism within this positivity: as soon as there is a presentation of the thing, I discover that this presentation emerges from out of a region that was previously unclear to me, and thus that the presentation occurs on the basis of a transcendence into alterity. To interrogate this alterity, on the other hand, is not to discover its originality or that the positive is in fact grounded by a negation. Neither does interrogation discover a transcendent "third" principle that mediates the positive and the negative. It discovers, rather, that the negativity behind the present plenum nevertheless refers to the present as that which is not immediately graspable by me. Thus, for Merleau-Ponty, the present plenum and its alterior ground do not stand at a distance from one another but rather each points back to a region in which they converge. He writes that the positive plenum and the negativism from out of which it arises are in fact "synonymous" and that, originally, "there is not the least divergence between them."[31]

That the present phenomenon in fact derives from out of the same region from whence its negativity derives implies that each term indexes a process of differentiation. Thus for Merleau-Ponty, too, there is always a basic polemic between the entity and the ground from which it arises. Yet this polemic, on Merleau-Ponty's view, is radicalized such that it does not indicate Being *as such* apart from beings but rather crosses out ontological difference. The polemic for Merleau-Ponty reveals a being that bears a definitive character of differentiation. Merleau-Ponty thus writes in his *Nature* course notes that a natural event is in fact the "privileged expression" of ontology and thus that we must understand an ontology only with reference to this event and not other to it.[32] He thus calls "[n]ature as a leaf or layer of total Being" in order to place nature within, as a co-constituent moment of, being.[33] To think of nature as a layer of being is to return to it a primacy and productive power of "ontological mutations."[34] This is more radical than the internal-connection between the natural event and being according to Heidegger's readings of *physis*. The problem that arises for Heidegger in his 1943 Epilogue to *What is Metaphysics?* thus does not arise in Merleau-Ponty's thought: only when there are beings can there be being, where being, rediscovered by Merleau-Ponty in its natural element, is defined only by differentiation.

Merleau-Ponty clarifies a basic ambivalence in Heidegger's meditations on *physis* and attempts to show that, in a more radical sense, being does *not* have an abiding meaning that stands apart, nor does it have a negativity that is distinct from differentiation. Merleau-Ponty writes of a "Being in promiscuity" in which "the in itself-for-itself integration takes place."[35] This promiscuity, he remarks elsewhere, allows for an "inaugural *there is*" that is, "no longer a question of origins, nor limits, nor of a series of events going to a first cause, but one sole *explosion* of Being which is *forever*."[36] There is no pure emergence of Being. Being is not a "first word" or a "pure instantiation," not a universal, general or fundamental order. It is defined by confliction, by the inherent collision between a multiformity of various orders. Being is, in other words, a primordial production, a *logos* that has a share in producing one thought by deforming and deviating from another. It thus exists only insofar as a present and explicit order stops short and shows its limits and gaps, its tendencies. It is present in the excessive claim of what must be said, heard, seen and is thus the un-sayable, the in-audible, or the in-visible.[37]

The relation of difference here – the un-sayable, the in-audible, the in-visible of the said, heard, seen – is not oppositional but conjunctive. Dufrenne suggests that the "and" in "Eye and Mind" or *The Visible and the Invisible* "cannot signify an opposition in any sense, not a dialectical relation, nor a relation of priority as in cause and effect, nor even as a relation of complimentarity as in form and content."[38] In his *Nature* course notes, for instance, Merleau-Ponty says that, "[t]here is no priority of effect over cause," and that "[i]t is impossible to distinguish . . . the meaning from the meaning where it is expressed."[39] The difference between what is expressed and the meaning it holds out is discovered in the very location of the expression. This location does not surpass itself in order to refer to an efficient cause that links all events together. Rather, it opens out into a power from out of which it has been articulated.

This chiasmic relation between what is explicitly expressed and that out of which the expressed emerges ultimately bears the structure of what Merleau-Ponty famously refers to as "flesh." The flesh, Merleau-Ponty writes in an oft-quoted passage, does not start "from substances, from body and spirit," nor is it "the union of contradictories."[40] It is, rather, a "concrete emblem of a general manner of being." The flesh is, in other words, an "incarnate principle" that determinates both contradictories.[41] It is thus intervallic, a genative realm hidden underneath and between things that has allowed them to originate. One could say that the flesh, for Merleau-Ponty, is older than even the first

Christian designation of it. It is not an origin *per se*, but rather, in the pre-Socratic sense of "*omou ēn panta*," the flesh is an *originating* of being.[42] The flesh, for Merleau-Ponty, thus makes reference to the archaic notion of the elements.[43] It "starts from water, air, earth, and fire, that is, in the sense of a *general thing*, midway between the spatio-temporal individual and the idea . . ."[44]

The work of art, insofar as it proceeds from out of this incarnated principle, brings into presence a region of existence that is prior to the active will of the subject as well as the inert material of the object. It occurs from within a being that is neither outside of time nor located in any one particular place. The artwork thus comes to be on the basis of a ground that refuses to be a foundational principle and yet, in reflecting this ground, it does so without turning this ground into a foundational principle. The artwork breaks with the semantic order of things in order to take itself as its own referent and to have only itself for the context of its appearing. It reveals itself to occur on the basis of an inner spectacle that is first of all a spectacle of itself, a spectacle that refers to itself insofar as it appears from out of itself, before it can become a spectacle of something outside of itself. In its self-referentiality, in other words, the artwork breaks with mundane appearances and the conceptual fixity of objectivities in order to gain the unique ability to reveal what Melreau-Ponty calls the "coming-to-itself of the visible" and the "autofigurative" ground that is implicit in visible things.[45] The colours of a painting, for instance, do not rival one another as if in a hierarchy or an order that is replaced and supplanted by another order until an Absolute one is reached. They in fact usurp an abstract system of essences and refer instead to the concrete location from out of which they have arisen in order to convey the incarnated principle that has made them possible.

The ground of the art object in fact resists the question, "What is art?" For such a question is already a reflective engagement with the artwork that presupposes an essential substratum. But the artwork's referral to its own incarnate grounds from out of which it appears problematizes the very form of the question. Here the work of art frees itself from the impositions of the reflective and essentializing question. It reveals itself as being nothing less than the question of its own possibility. It reveals itself in its beginning, and continues to exist only as a questioning of its own beginnings. If the artwork begins with the question concerning its possibility, then it has no essence as yet. It exists as an absence of the reflective form of question, "What is art?"

The work of art's connection to flesh finally calls into question the very notion of form, placing the work back in touch with the incarnation of its own appearing. The most we can say about the ground of the artwork here is that, by taking only itself as its referent and in thus distancing itself from the mundane thing, it reveals itself to have emerged from out of an apparitional force that belongs to all things. The work thereby exposes nothing but the unrest of a movement that has no beginning and no end. Finally, the artwork's self-intimate questioning of its beginnings severely dismantles any claim to form and essence. It reveals not a univocal being but, under the name of depth, of space, of colour, conveys instead a "system of equivalences, a *Logos* of lines, of lighting, of colours, of reliefs, of masses."[46] The artwork is nothing less than the revelation of the lack of absolute grounds in order to operate at the elision of unthematic meanings that are always already internal to the things themselves.

Nature and Art: Interrogating Formal Structure

I am concerned in this section only with the natural being, to which the artwork refers back, which undercuts the work's formal aspects and technical procedures, specifically, point, line, colour. The point, line and colour inevitably dissolve form, for Merleau-Ponty, and as I will show in the following section this dissolution of form is what comes to haunt the image by ultimately exposing a process prior to technical procedures, which Merleau-Ponty will call "desire."

Point. The origin of the image, as we began to see in the last chapter, involves a hand extending out into an incarnated principle of appearing that calls into question a transcendental ground of the artwork. This incarnate principle of appearing shows that the artwork does not originate from out of a perspective projection in which the relation between seer and the seen corresponds to a point-occupancy system in space and time. Coming into being on the basis of a field-structure that contains the possibilities of arrangements for the image, the artwork's originary mode of existing betrays a natural being that in fact renders obsolete a system of space and time. Its mode of being exposes, in turn, a more primal logic from out of which and within which natural events occur in time.

Merleau-Ponty most explicitly treats the activity of painterly work in the light of a natural being in his *Nature* course notes. There he equates the Matisse film in which the painter "threw his brush in as many diverse places as possible, and after a certain time, logic appeared" with "an accelerated film of the growth of a flower" in which "movement appears as a particular case of growth."[47] The flower's growth does not follow an "already made trajectory" but a "trajectory that is going to follow."[48] We cannot understand growth to obey some esoteric logic. It is rather a becoming of *logos* in relation only to the being that grows.[49] This means that for the growing being,

each moment of its history is empty of what will follow, an emptiness which will be filled later . . . we observe that there is the future in every present, because its present is in a state of imbalance. The rupture of equilibrium appears as an operant non-being, which impedes the organism from staying in the anterior phase. It is only a question of an absence, but an absence of what? That's what is difficult to know. There is no solution in the strict sense . . .[50]

The growing being emerges from out of a growth that has no solution, since it is not merely the notion of lack or conceptualized absence. Growth, then, is not something that the growing being needs to fulfil in advance of itself. In this sense, growth is not a specific in-itself *other* to the growing being but rather a productive power in general that continually ruptures the equilibrium of the thing.[51] What the gestures of Matisse reveal, according to Merleau-Ponty, is precisely this productive and rupturing power. His gestures, for instance, convey a logic that is the realm of all possible movement that is opened up by the one specific gesture. But this logic is not opened until then.

One could say that, insofar as it operates on the basis of what Merleau-Ponty calls growth, Matisse's brushwork reveals a "place" no longer in the sense of a location of mass in space but rather in the original and primal sense of *topos* in which a thing comes to be, to occupy space, on the basis of its place.[52] The brushwork does not calculate in advance of its extension a previously conceived and fixed point in space but rather opens up anew a space that circumscribes the place of the movement. The painter's stroke extends through space only insofar as this space first relates to a concrete movement. The event of creation, consequently, involves an interplay between space and the concrete movement of the painter's stroke. The work of art thus calls into question the very notion of a point-occupancy system since it originates from out of a logic that is prior to any such system.

In *L'institution, La passivité*, Merleau-Ponty speaks of the growth of geometry underneath a planarmetric perspective.[53] In "Eye and Mind," he writes of "the modes of space" or the "prosaic space" in which space "radiates around planes that cannot be assigned to any place at all."[54] A prosaic space defies fixity. It cannot be assigned to any one specific place because it is assigned to all places in the sense that it is relieved in all places. Thus the entity in the work of art cannot be understood to occupy space in the sense of the singular point; and neither is space a container for a set of points belonging to it. A prosaic space is not possible without its reliefs and masses. A long Working Note in the *Visible and the Invisible* reiterates and expands this specific sense of space, relating it primarily to a *topos*:

> The Euclidean space is the model for perspectival being . . . Underlying appropriateness of this idea of space (and of velocity, movement, time) with the classical ontology of the *Ens realissimum*, of the infinite entity. The topological space, on the contrary, a milieu in which are circumscribed relations of proximity, of envelopment, etc. is the image of a being that, like Klee's touches of colour, is at the same time older than everything and "of the first day" (Hegel) . . . It is encountered not only at the level of the physical world, but again it is constitutive of life, and finally it founds the *wild* principle of Logos – It is this wild or brute being that intervenes at all levels to overcome the problems of the classical ontology (mechanism, finalism . . .)[55]

This is a particularly dense Working Note, to be sure. There is of course a reference to the colour theory of Paul Klee, to which we will return below. For the moment, a prosaic-cum-topological space is to be contrasted with a Euclidean space. The latter marks the advent of an idealistic meaning within space. It posits the phenomenon of space as an occurrence defined by a set of qualities. This positing allows perspective to relate to the angle from which an object is seen.[56] Thus, space, from the Euclidean perspective – the perspective that a Renaissance *skēnographia* and Cartesian optics would later privilege – is to be understood on the basis of geometrical light rays (*lumen*). A prosaic or topological space, on the other hand, does not idealize perspective nor does it forsake the concrete. Rather than understanding space and the perspective within that space as angular, the prosaic or topological space of the artwork refers back to the same space that is opened up only in relation to a bodily movement that is in transit through it. The artwork, in other words, conveys the very same space that has been opened up by the singular movement and has allowed the passage of that singular movement.

The artwork thus reveals a profound reversal of transcendence. The prosaic or topological transcendence from out of which the work originates exists not in the self-identity of perspective. It does not originate from out of a transcendence of space that, because it has been theorized as an "infinite entity" in itself, is seen from an angle. The topological or prosaic space of the artwork is rather defined as an auto-dispersion underneath perspective in which we grasp the "circumscribed relations of proximity" between things and space, or the "envelopment" of things by a space that works itself between and around those things. This is what Merleau-Ponty calls a radiation, dimension or world-ray in which each thing extends into a depth that inwardly binds them together. One should not understand a prosaic or topological transcendence that inwardly binds things to convey a static dimension. That would imply that topological space is a utopia, which, although it has no real locality and is literally a no-where (*eu-topos*), affords consolation by opening up an untroubled region behind the things.[57] It could imply, alternatively, that a topological space is a "heterotopia" that, as an extraordinary order, existing elsewhere, desiccates words by stopping them in their tracks and contesting the very possibility of any language at all, let alone the value of its contours.[58] Adapting the phraseology of Visker and Waldenfels, one should rather say that a prosaic or topological space is in fact "radically atopic."[59] That is, a topological space is always, and every-where, in the act of taking form in relation to any concrete particular. It is not a space that transcends things in the sense of existing apart from them. As atopic, it could be said, the relation of transcendence between the thing and its space reveals an interrogative effort to convey the concrete being inasmuch as it is not "denatured" and "silhouetted" against an original negativity that defines it. The rela-tion of transcendence between the thing and its space also reveals a nullity that is not denatured insofar as it is always activated in relation to the concrete being. The thing reaches out into negativity, is pro-longed into the depth of this negativity, while this negativity is only the negative in relation to the concrete thing and thus in need of a specific placement.

This transcendence of topological or prosaic space, especially as a world-ray, must reference an alternate form of light that arises from the concrete. The notion of light conveyed by a concrete space must allow the now illuminated thing to arise from out of a now dimmed background – a foreground standing against a real background. This is light understood as *lux*, as the rediscovery of the unmediated (direct) assimilation of an external, physical world in which we dis-cover the very sensuousness of light. *Lux* is the light that flashes and brings about apparitions, itself non-apparent and invisible. It is "with-out fiat, without creator, subject or source" since "it is the source but in itself refracted, in itself radiant, exploding, broken."[60]

In the lecture course, "Philosophy and Non-Philosophy Since Hegel," Merleau-Ponty speaks of a "new idea of light."[61] This light, he says, obeys a sort of "pharisaism" in its disclosure of the relation between subject and object. It bears a structure of accordance between subject and object that is not grasped by means of an external logic of this relation. The relation is in fact denied when one affirms or claims it, and thus affirmation itself cannot be its establishment. Rather than bearing the structure of univocity, then, this new idea of light brings to bear a meaning of "the true" that is polysemic and mul-tiple (Merleau-Ponty uses the word "*Vieldeutigkeit*").[62] It understands light from the perspective of a concrete and sensuous content. Light, as *lux*, is literally spatial. It is really *there*, Merleau-Ponty points out in his institution course notes.[63] It no longer connotes the neutrality of a geometrical and ideal region but rather an investment of one's eye in the concrete. It allows us to see a true light, in other words, where "the true cannot be defined as coincidence and outside of all difference in relation to the true."[64] It allows us to return to a light that bears the concrete polemic between the clear and the dim. The shadow, Merleau-Ponty says, does not eliminate a true light.[65] He writes in *Signs* that there is instead a "chiaroscuro of the *doxa*" in which a world is revealed through its "dissimulation."[66] This polemic is what Caravaggio once again liberates in his assault on Renaissance illusionism; figures on a Caravaggio canvas emerge from out of their previous dimness in order to be illuminated. What is seen is thus an opening up; and what is not seen, too, is concrete rather than ideal, for it too may very well come into appearance. It is this light for Caravaggio that gives the things their phenomenality. Caravaggio can thus be linked with what Merleau-Ponty in the institution course notes calls the depiction of world, rather than perspective, in antiquity painting.[67]

Line. The grapheme, as the mark of the painter's movement, is not merely a mechanical or technical element of the work. The painter's singular movement, in this context of a prosaic or topological space, is always a movement through and partaking a dimension that is other to it. Yet it is also by passing through this alterior space that the painter comes to herself. This openness is (and this will be important in the last section of this chapter, on desire) just an openness to the volitional structure, to the field of activity and affectivity. It reveals a remarkable interplay between ipseity and alterity, between interiority and exteriority, between the *Innen* and *Aussenleiblichkeit*.

Merleau-Ponty must first resist da Vinci's *Treatise on Painting* in which the painter, equating painting with philosophy, claims that the line simply re-presents the mathematical algorithms of the things seen. "The secret of the art of drawing," Merleau-Ponty writes, "is to discover in each object the particular way in which a certain flexuous line, which is, so to speak, its generating axis, is direct through its whole extent."[68] The flexuous line discovers a generating axis: a brushstroke generates one possible planarity only when it stretches through space and time. The formulated line does not interrupt anything, for Merleau-Ponty. Nor does it establish a new or different order of space that belongs solely to the artwork and that cuts itself off, qua aesthetic object, from its surrounding world. To say that the line betrays a mobile that is identical to a uniformity of all movements across a space and time, identical across all phases of movement, this is already a thematization of the certain mobility betrayed by the line. The painterly line is the mark of a certain mobile, or even *movens*, which is the unity of a singular movement; this one *movens* is simply that which remains identical to itself, and no other, in the phase of its own movement. The line is a figuration of a *movens* that moves not by reason of its static properties but by its behaviour. It is the mark of movement only of one and the same *movens*, of one and the same appearing thing, of a single something that makes itself known through itself.

The painterly line is not anti-logical, but it remains proto-logical or pre-logical. It expresses a transit of the brushwork that has *taken place* and thus requires an alterity that appears only after the stroke has happened. The painted line, that is, passes through the spatiality of a pre-objective being that defies univocity. It is not the expression of a geometrical or physical space but the expression of a spatiality that continually appears and that precedes objective space, defined in each use by the familiar grasp of the painter's body on its world. Every line thus presupposes a secret activity by which, for the first time, is worked out an original being-in the environment. Nevertheless, Merleau-Ponty says, even if the line submits to this pre-thematic space, it also expresses a "value of a curvature of space."[69] How can a *value* at the same time express an unthematic and pre-objective logic? How can the painter, as Merleau-Ponty puts it, "let a line muse" for being?[70]

The line, for Merleau-Ponty, emerges on the basis of an unthematic projection in order to convey the thing as hovering, floating, modulating or undulating rather than a flat planarity.[71] The line no longer conveys, "the apparition of an entity upon a vacant background, as it was in classical geometry," but a background that subtends and is everywhere circumabulating the entity.[72] It transcends beyond itself and brings into exposition a prosaic or topological space that concretely relates to the formulations of the thing. The thing is thus not merely the outline, shape or dead envelope but is always already imbued with an internal suggestiveness and incompletion. It in fact restores to the thing its internal metaphoricity. Merleau-Ponty writes that the line is "the prosaic definition [*signalement*] of the entity and the hidden [*sourde*] operation which composes in it such softness or inertia and such force as are required to constitute it *as nude, as face, as flower*."[73] "Matisse's women," he says elsewhere in that same passage, referring to drawings such as *Standing Nude with Downcast Eyes* or *Head of a Recumbent Figure*, "were not immediately women; they became women" on account of their "constitutive emptiness."[74]

The line indicates a primal transcending, for Merleau-Ponty. "Drawing," Paul Klee famously said, "is taking the line for a walk." It needs to stray and free itself from the thing. No longer confined to the envelope of the thing, the line is directed instead to its hidden movement by conveying a bodily intention, underneath the visible thing, of a pre-given logic. This logic is the apparitional force inherent within the thing. While the line opens up and is a sort of suggestive mark towards this logic, still the painting is, as Merleau-Ponty says in "Indirect Language and the Voices of Silence" in reference to Van Gogh's *The Crows*, a "going farther."[75] It more than suggests. It makes one confront the suggestion itself, and in this sense it confers into visibility "what still must be done in order to restore the encounter between his glance and the things which solicit it."[76] This is a sort of restoration of possibility, a bringing into existence what has never in fact been. The painting confers onto the canvas a coming-into-presence, and this is done, for Merleau-Ponty, by colouration. In this sense, the particular colour does not merely show the appearance in the way it has appeared but, more exactly, it shows the wild *logos* inherent to the phenomenon arising into the open from out of itself.

Colour. Merleau-Ponty writes of the "objects inserted in the rhythm of colour."[77] This rhythm, Galen Johnson notes, "is an order that does not totalize, an order of possibilities filled with risk rather than algorithm at the edge of necessity, for this is the order of natality."[78] The logic of colour is that of emergence: the specific colour belongs to the visible thing – the red, blue, yellow, etc. – but invariably our eye, moving beyond specificity, sinks towards that from out of which the colour germinates. The painting, qua painting, makes us see not merely the red, blue or yellow things but a colouration that allows each specific colour to arise as such. This dimension of colouration is the now opened range of actual and possible relations:

> Now this particularity of the colour, of the yellow, and this univer-
> sality are not a *contradiction*, are *together* sensoriality itself: it is by the
> same virtue that the colour, the yellow, at the same time gives itself
> as a *certain* being and as a *dimension*, the expression of every *possible*
> being.[79]

Each colour, for Merleau-Ponty, expresses a relation between the apparent things on the basis of some internal region of convergence or interplay. The balance and imbalance between colours, the equilibrium and disequilibrium of colour relations, these can subsume the measure of the line and the weight of shading and generate the possibility of what Paul Klee calls the "subconscious dimension of the picture."[80] It is colour, then, that expresses a depth or profundity from out of which beings arise, a dimension in which things no longer have opposing shapes set against one another but participate in one and the same sensoriality. This dimension of colouration is what unveils the being as that which is not "beyond all latency and all depth, having no true thickness [*épasseur*]."[81] It breaks the "skin of things" and displays "how the things become things, how the world becomes world."[82] The logic of colour, finally, shows how one world appears from the depths, and in this sense it is an excavation of another possible meaning among the proposed, now appearing meaning. We might say that, through the dimension of colouration, the painting offers us a suggested meaning rather than a commanded one. It is in suggesting rather than commanding that the painting betrays the logic of a polymorphic[83] and deflagrated[84] being that does not *create* things so much as it allows things to *form themselves*.[85]

It is true, however, that Merleau-Ponty's obsession with Cézanne in "Cézanne's Doubt" is primarily because the voluminosity of his canvases reveals a certain univocity, a Gestalt in which particulars are combined and inserted into a totality that subordinates them. In this case, the depth concealed at the canvas' surface implies a hidden dimension in which objects and their shapes and colouration compete with one another as "branches," but of one, singular Being. For instance, one of the canvases on which Merleau-Ponty reflects in "Cézanne's Doubt," *Nature Morte avec Pommes*, portrays objects sharing the same colours intermingled. From the greyish shadow of a plate, mixed largely with ultramarine and white and a complimentary vermilion to dim the hue's intensity, to the greyish tone in the tablecloth, again mixed primarily with white, ultramarine, vermilion and also chrome yellow, the painting displays a world with little spatial recession, teeming with dense objectivities that are all strangely competing with one another in my field of vision. Differing little from the foreground to the background, the brushwork does nothing to relieve this. It at least tries to rethink the logical relation between the things and to evoke their internal linkage to one another, to exhibit a structure of being that translates itself into the visibility of lines, colour, movement.

But by the time Merleau-Ponty writes "Eye and Mind," his description of Cézanne's *Portrait of Vallier* is specifically aimed at deflagration: the painting, he writes, "sets white spaces between the colours which take on the function of giving shape to, and setting off, a being more general than yellow-being or green-being or blue-being."[86] Cézanne's last paintings often leave white patches in order to allow them to come alive with the movement of nature and lay bare the painstaking process by which he translated the original shaping and setting of things. These white spaces, dormant between colours, indeed interlock particular events but now also characterize them with a kind of singularity. Particular beings such as a yellow-being, a green-being or a blue-being are no longer simply subsumed by an individual gestalt-moment in the Cézanne but are rather specific open points of access with particular linkages that multiply, branch out, interweave and still ultimately reach back to the nullity of being that shines forth when the particulars are absorbed into their white spaces. These spaces are in a sense determinate, it is true, but they function by *determinating* particulars and are thus essential for Cézanne to convey nature's movement.

Because of these white spaces, one notices that in one of the portraits of Vallier (there were three, beginning from the end of 1905 or the beginning of 1906) that Vallier, Cézanne's garden keeper at the time, is painted in similar colours and with similar handling as is *Le Cabanon de Jourdan*, which is said to be the painter's last landscape and is no longer a classical view of nature but rather verges on dissolving into indeterminate abstraction. Vallier sits in profile, arms crossed, against the wall of Cézanne's garden, over which we can just barely see a view of green and what seems to be refracted light. There is a shadowy outline against Vallier's back but, again, this does nothing to give the canvas any spatial recession so much as it makes the gardener appear in the midst of wood and moss, brick and mortar, and the sense of strangeness in the back, all of which fall back into particular gaps. We might say that Vallier's body, like the apples of the *Nature Morte* described above, "swells" and has no exact location.[87] But in the portrait, in particular, this lack is precisely what gives Vallier shape and so it is this formative lack that is made explicit. The painting "is a spectacle of something," writes Merleau-Ponty, "only by being a spectacle of nothing . . ."[88] Vallier's body, since it is emergent and determinated by something indeterminate, *is* perhaps on display, but more so in the sense of *displicare*, which in Latin means "to scatter" or "to disperse" and in Medieval Latin even means "to unfold," and has the sense of something deploying itself.

The primacy of colouration is nowhere more evident for Merleau-Ponty than in the canvases of Paul Klee. Klee's "touches of colours" do betray a totality of regions – the painting as a whole as perceived from the privileged position – that commands and governs. But this privileged position must be qualified, for it arises only where each region of colour is its own centre of gravity and locus of rest or arrest. The touch of colour is thus a calculated place for mediation and consummation.[89] It comes forward on the canvas in order to express its penetration into a general colouration. Klee writes in *On Modern Art* of his tireless attempts at "pure drawing," or "painting in pure tone values," his pursuit to "work out methods of painting in coloured tone values, in complementary colours, in multicolours and methods of total colour painting."[90] He notes that he has tried "combining and again combining" these methods of colour in order to "preserve the culture of the pure element."[91] But "nothing can be rushed," he ultimately says. "It must grow, it should grow of itself . . . We must go on seeking it!"[92] The utter laboriousness of the touch of colour subsumes the formal aspects of the composition while at the same time for Klee it seeks to express the meaning of an object, and its style.

The formal aspects are consequently in service of Klee's colours that, as Merleau-Ponty says, "seem[s] to have been born slowly upon the canvas, to have emanated from some primordial ground"[93] This ground, finally, possesses a basic indecidability at its core. Colouration shows us a *logos* as it scatters between the formalities of perspectival seeing – a *logos* as it comes forward, not before or after but *now*, a constant renewing.

Desire and Art: Interrogating Content

In the *Physics*, Aristotle calls *atopos* (which literally means "*hors-lieu*" or "out of place") such an "absurd" concept "that the point would be void." According to Merleau-Ponty, however, the artwork makes a claim on this basically non-philosophical understanding of transcendence since it exposes a prosaic or topological space into which the self opens. There is a transcendence, according to Merleau-Ponty, that surrounds us and escapes us with all of its thickness and depth. But, in doing so, this transcendence is not a principled condition of inexhaustibility: we are demitted and prevented from turning back onto the self only because it is through this transcendence that we become a self. This primal transcendence in fact subtends the two far apart topologies of the self and the world. These topologies would be antimonous, in fact, were they not both understood on the basis of an elemental or natural being.

It is important to note, then, that for Merleau-Ponty natural being also conveys an implicit transcendence of the self that contains no thematic or explicit meaning but rather an unthematic meaning or what he calls "desire." The insight that desire is, fundamentally, a structuration of being is not exactly new. It is what is discovered, we could say, after the phenomenological analysis of intentionality and the radical questioning of its limits. In the *Logical Investigations*, for instance, Husserl describes intentionality as the satisfaction of bringing the previous dissatisfaction of empty intentions into relief. Intentional consciousness is thus fundamentally in need of an affective component created by the limitedness or incompleteness of an object's givenness and by the object's appearance against the background of a manifold. The recent works by Renaud Barbaras (*Desire and Distance: Introduction to a Phenomenology of Perception*[94]) and Galen Johnson (*The Retrieval of the Beautiful: Thinking Through Merleau-Ponty's Aesthetics*[95]) show just how deeply Merleau-Ponty's analyses of desire are informed by this structure of pre-intentionality. It is as if the intentional object is "split in two," Johnson writes.[96] It "provides satisfaction" when it is intended.[97] But this satisfaction occurs on the basis of a "sudden incompleteness,"[98] that is, on the basis of a tending towards something that is fundamentally tension and expectation. What is truly the object of desire, then, is not any object as such but what is beneath the surface of that object. Here desire is distinguished from need of the particular, for it opens up to the alterity subtending the particular on the basis of which it appears. Desire is desire for the fullness of the presence of the invisibility from out of which the visible unfolds. It travels what Merleau-Ponty calls an "open circuit," which brings into play different possible gazes and bodies from one's own.[99]

This, in turn, opens up Merleau-Ponty's radical claim about the structure of desire: originally, there is no self-absorbed desire that requires a dialectic. Desire, for Merleau-Ponty, does not in the first instance require sublimating in order to mediate two individuals (e.g., Hegel, Sartre). It does not need to be raised into a third term apart from two individuals that only then negotiates them. In fact, one should note that what Merleau-Ponty calls "the silent labour of desire"[100] explicitly undermines the communion between *algos* (pain and labour) and *logos* that exists for Hegel. The labour of desire, for Merleau-Ponty, is the very logic of phenomenality coming into presence. This desire refers instead to a more foundational operant logic, beneath the appearance of objects, that catches up individuals inside of it. One could perhaps say that desire for Merleau-Ponty is what in phenomenality concretely structures individuals while at the same time allowing for a relation between them. The repression of desire that is said to take place in the form of service, work, culture, is thus in fact a setting of what Merleau-Ponty calls desire into motion. This can be seen in his notion of style, in which an artist sets out to express in terms of the visible, and yet inevitably expresses a process that is not at all her own and prior to her expression. This inevitability is not so much the result of an activity on the part of the painter so much as it results from out of a transcendence that is not a different category of existence from her own. More basic than the explicit attempt at expression, then, what invariably gets expressed indirectly is a structure, other to the conscious will to express, that has allowed the particular expression to come into the world. It is this indirectly indicated structure in the explicit expression that Merleau-Ponty locates as desire. One notices that, already in this desire, there is a moment of repression that, although it announces itself as alter to the painter, still does not take the painter away from the sensible site in which it occurs.

The created work of art, I want to say here, thus conveys the present expression as co-originating, in the sensible world, alongside what is absent from it. Here the artwork brings into being the very structure of desire that upholds the difference between what is presently indicated and what, underneath this presentation, is not. It displays the very emergence of desire, beyond explicit meaning, alive to the logic that determines or differentiates particulars, and thus, in a profound sense, to nothing less than natural being itself. Merleau-Ponty does indicate that the artwork, in its inner-relation with natural being, exhibits the structure of a passionate desire. In "Eye and Mind," for instance, he speaks of the "deflagration" of being, which at once characterizes both the explosion and fragmentation of being into the interstices of various things and allows the painter to *burn* in the act of painting.[101] It is precisely this burning that restores to the visible world an invisibility by which the painter has been touched. In a more indirect reference to the element of air, Merleau-Ponty famously writes the following: "There really is inspiration and expiration of Being, respiration in Being, action and passion so slightly discernible that it becomes impossible to distinguish between . . . who paints and what is painted."[102]

That the artwork betrays a bind between desire and the natural being of the phenomenon implies, for Merleau-Ponty, that there is no need to choose between the real and the fictive. So-called representations of the real are always already opened out into a structure of desire that allows for the possibility of representations. They are thus never really literal since they ultimately concern themselves with giving access to a concrete condition of possibility of things. The fictive, in turn, never truly departs from the logic of appearances since it emerges from out of this non-factuality or non-literality inherent to

the appearing of the thing. In this sense, the artwork not only operates on the basis of an implicit bind between desire and the natural
being of the phenomenon but confers this co-generation into
existence by bringing to the light of day the hitherto unexpressed
meaning underneath the thing that has in fact never really been.
The figure is structured not by the real but by the compelling force
in the natural process of appearing in the appearance. We could
say that the things conveyed by the artwork let-appear this force of
compellation.

In front of Goya's *Nude Maja*, for instance, a viewer is less likely to
be moved by a supernatural beauty to the figure so much as by a
beauty that already submits to the weight of a flexuous body pressing
into the density of the green velvet that stands out against darkness.
One is also attracted by the very figurations of Maja's incarnation,
which puts an otherwise unreal and inaccessible beauty in play,
making it tangible. Fascination begins not with the impossible as
such, but in the softening lines that convey the possibility of being
caressed. This softening is itself a sensitivity for the concrete, for the
tenderness, fragility, vulnerability and availability to touch. It is a
sensitivity of limitedness and frailty, and the nude's figurations are
vulnerable only in tension with what threatens to overflow the fragile
form from inside out. The fragility of the nude, in other words, relies
on an ambiguity between an exorbitant nudity and an excess of
visibility and a hitherto unexpressed meaning that is too volatile to
uphold itself without being figured into visibility. The visible requires
the eruption of the previously unexpressed, for Merleau-Ponty, and in
every non-figurative spectacle there belies the fictive and unthematic.

Merleau-Ponty writes that, "in laying out its oneiric universe of
carnal essences, painting mixes the imaginary and the real."[103] The
artwork, for Merleau-Ponty, not only allows things to figure an impulse
towards those things but also denies that things and the impulse
towards them are separate categories. The thing conveyed by the artwork can function symbolically, then, only because it opens up that
symbolic possibility. Later, in my final chapter, I will say more about
how Merleau-Ponty consequently thinks of what he calls a "figured
philosophy" of painting that fundamentally mixes the real and the
symbolic.[104] I only wish now to examine how the artwork reveals for

him objectivities as they open up and even contain unconscious contents. Merleau-Ponty will ultimately want to say that the object conveyed by the artwork is symbolic because of a transgression of its particular object-hood but not because of a transgression of its temporality. In fact, it is this indexed temporality, according to him, that will allow the object to operate indeterminately and symbolically. Both the object as well as the repressed unconscious for which it functions as a symbol will thus have to be understood in terms of a symbolic functioning that is not reducible to either term. At this point, then, the symbolic functioning of the object must be repositioned in the context of a significance that operates in both the object and in the act of repression. This more latent process of significance is what the artwork confers.

This thesis that there is a fundamental lack of conceptual fixity in the symbolic structure is already implicated in Merleau-Ponty's dealings with Freud's famous essay on Leonardo's childhood memories in "Cézanne's Doubt." There Merleau-Ponty calls into question the basic assumption in reading Freud that the depicted objects in Leonardo's work are dialectically opposite from the structures of the unconsciousness for which those objects operate as a symbol, and thus that the painted objects in fact betray a fixed structure that can be understood before them.[105] The artwork, for Merleau-Ponty, fundamentally denies the representational assumption that there is a static ontological structure prior to the depiction. Though a real and specific concrete referent may in some sense be represented in the work of art, at the same time this referent can only betray for Merleau-Ponty an *ambiguity or indeterminacy* that applies in advance of the object. If for Merleau-Ponty the thing in the artwork functions symbolically, then, its symbolic functioning is in fact fundamentally indeterminated – both in advance of its being conferred onto a canvas and afterward. Furthermore, for Merleau-Ponty, this indeterminacy inherent to the symbolic is not a structure of the psyche so much as it is a base structuration of the thing.

The artwork thus *brings into existence* the symbolic functioning of an object. That the artwork brings into existence this functioning of the thing implies that the artwork, at least implicitly, shows how the thing itself is, at its core, an indirection. The apparently real, that is, explicitly

given, referent in the artwork does not simply give an explicit meaning but also indirectly refers to a mode or manner in which it has
appeared. This particular mode of appearing acquires a symbolic
function in the artwork not because of a functioning that exists out of
necessity prior to the depicted object, or because the childhood
memories of Leonardo precede the object so that a symbolic functioning may then be conferred into the artwork. As a mode of appearing, and not merely as the simple outward shape of the thing, the
depicted object in the artwork conveys an otherwise implicit act of
formation in the phenomenality of the thing, its very *coming into
appearance*, from out of which the thing compels a certain unconscious meaning. Unconscious contents, for Merleau-Ponty, are in this
sense structured by the thing in the act of coming into appearance
and do not exist in advance of and apart from things.[106] I would go
so far as to suggest here that, in revealing not things but their compelling force over the painter in the very formation of their appearance, the artwork reveals what Freud, referring to both sexual and
artistic pleasure, calls an "incitement premium." That is, the artwork
conveys the "fore-pleasure" in which one takes pleasure in the coming-
to-pleasure. It is only that, for Merleau-Ponty, this fore-pleasure is
structured by phenomenality in the recurrent act of forming itself.

There is the obvious problem here for Merleau-Ponty of having
to recharacterize officially accepted readings of, say, the paintings of
Henri Michaux or Salvador Dali, who explicitly aim to collapse painterly vision and break radically from existence, or the images of
Picasso that intentionally fragment the world. It could be pointed
out, for instance, that the cubist work requires an explicit act in order
to show a fore-pleasure that is *in direct conflict* with normative meanings.
This is why the cubist image freely effaces the realistic image with the
use of multiple, contradictory light sources. It is a very conscious pursuit of a new aesthetic that highlights the *descensus ad infernum*, the
undaunted, explicit invocation of so-called primitive conflicts.[107] In
this invocation it is said that the Picasso canvas marks a resistance
of the painter both against a sensible world that is "unmanned"
and against a psyche that is "unsouled." It "tears open the mouth
of humanity," in order to rediscover the so-called savage, which is
"greater than the threat of nature," an "inner redeeming power."[108]

We could also say that this new revelation of the savage, following Lyotard's renderings of the artwork, allows the art object to convey a fundamental discontinuity between the primitive conflicts of a psyche and existence. No matter what the work displays, then, it inevitably conveys a "mute experience of 'I without a self' audible without violating its silence" and is "the discipline of listening before-beyond the audible, of sensitizing itself to that which is insensitive to it."[109] The art object is essentially non-objective, and this means that it can never put into play the force of the signified of things and is always, rather, a form or plastic organization of the figural in reality. For Lyotard in *Discours, Figure* this means that the work belongs to the category of transgression. It transgresses the object, and it transgresses space. Thus we need to pay attention to the work as a product of dissonance. For the work is always a "deconciliation."[110] It is always "constituted as a network of discontinuities."[111] It only ever inscribes libidinal energies into the real in order to reveal them as apart from the real.

Merleau-Ponty has to show that an ignorance of the real, such as Picasso's, is not more than the suspense of a naturalistic gaze and the discovery of a transgression already implicit to the appearing object. The disjointedness and juxtapositions of a Picasso thus break with the object only insofar as they render with greater eloquence the *descensus ad infernum* that the external shape of the object implicitly has in store. Since Merleau-Ponty understands this confliction in reference to the very phenomenality of the thing, the thing as a phenomenon in the act of taking form, he can in fact accept the premise of cubism to extend the contrast of shadow and light beyond its traditional function of merely translating the sculptural quality of objects. For Merleau-Ponty as well, the play of light sources and the line in relation to these sources reveals the visible thing as it moves out into a non-objective and unthematic meaning in order to render the constant confliction that is endemic to the un-conscious.

Merleau-Ponty's critical argument against Lyotard's treatment of the art object, however, comes in reference to the artwork's inauguration. The event of creation does not reveal the un-real into the real on the basis of a dissonance. It must be recalled here that for Merleau-Ponty the artwork acquires a power to open up the unconscious meanings of things because it first arises from out of a hand that acts as a "conductor" or mediator between painting and the invisibility of things.[112] The painter's gesture that inaugurates one order, we have already seen, must also displace and suppress some other possible gesture and its possible order that would articulate meaning in some other way.[113] The primitive conflict that the artwork displays, for Merleau-Ponty, is not a conflict belonging to the human but rather a conflict inherent to natural being into which the hand must extend in order to convey the one meaning. The artwork is thus symbolic of what Merleau-Ponty calls the open structure of desire, which is open on the basis of this exteriorization of the artist, and unfinished on the basis of an unending conflict of orders belonging to natural being into which the artist is exteriorized.

It is thus important for Merleau-Ponty that we take to heart Paul Klee's repeated saying that the trees look at him, or Cézanne's declaration that when the mountain of Sainte-Victoire looks at him it reveals itself as the visual incoherence of an uprising mass.[114] It is the painter who gives himself over, exposing the place in which he is exteriorized not by specific things but by the hidden "encroachment" or chiasmatic "interweaving" underneath them.[115] Specifically it is the painter who allows desire to come into existence just as it co-emerges along with an incoherent principle as it arises into the mass of things. Here the painter's desire is as an organizing principle in the apparition of things, interweaving those things, before it is even the painter's own. What the painter reveals is that, although this desire is inhuman, still it is not a different category apart from the human since the interweaving underneath particular things that structures this desire is the same interweaving into which the painter is exteriorized. Thus the artwork for Merleau-Ponty does in fact originate out of a transgression: the event of creation transgresses the categories of interior and exterior on the basis of a basic process underneath both terms, which Merleau-Ponty calls "desire"; and consequently the art object functions, according to Merleau-Ponty, to expose this fundamental openness. The latter is what Merleau-Ponty calls a "visible to the second power," a visible thing with a sort of power to extend beyond its visibility in order to show the invisible *as invisible*, that is, as coming into appearance before the artist.[116]

One can also address this lack of a break or rupture in desire between the inhuman and the human world of art in the terms announced by Merleau-Ponty at the beginning of *The Visible and the Invisible*. There Merleau-Ponty points out that the real is always already imbued with phantasy. This can be discovered, in fact, in the initial moments of doing phenomenology. The way to phenomenology, as a consistent maintenance of doubting in the service of comeditation and critique, already implies, as Merleau-Ponty points out in the opening passages of *The Visible and the Invisible*, that we never really do locate the inherent and essential difference between real perception and dreams.[117] Instead, we discover that,

> [a]s soon as we cease thinking of perception as the action of the pure physical object on the human body, and the perceived as the "interior" result of this action, it seems that every distinction between the true and the false, between methodic knowledge and phantasms, between science and the imagination, is ruined.[118]

The difference between perception and phantasy is not ever absolute. Rather, the two terms require some grounding in the same "ontological function" that above all lets us count both perception and dream as "among our experiences."[119] Both perception and phantasy are grounded by an ontological thickness and thus, foundationally, there is "no absolute contrast between the imaginary and the sensible."[120] This same thickness inherent to both perception and phantasy is already anticipated in Merleau-Ponty's claim that the latter is related to the fabric of intentional acts, which are previously hidden, unexpressed, repressed. Perception in fact marks a "return to a prepersonal relation to the world" and thus it allows us to question the "cleavage between the real and the imaginary." In this sense, he writes, "our waking relationships with objects have an oneiric character as a matter of principle . . . in the way dreams are, the way myths are . . ."[121] Merleau-Ponty's claim that perception and phantasy relate to one another through the same ontological ground implies that neither arise from out of the activity of a subject but rather they are opened out in some basic way to a reality that is already encountered as significant.[122]

Merleau-Ponty's provocative discovery is that intentions of phantasy and desire are in fact the result of a passivity that in turn opens out into a fundamental temporality hidden underneath the things of the world. Since for Merleau-Ponty it is this fundamental temporality that gives the thing its oneiric and symbolic character he will also say that the repressed unconscious for which this thing has significance must in turn also be understood on the basis of this temporality. Repression, in other words, travels a path beyond the thing and into a temporality that gives the things its symbolic significance. Significance is thus, more deeply, the result of the thing as an event happening in the midst of an indistinct, operant temporal succession. In the 1954 lectures notes, *L'institution, La passivite*, Merleau-Ponty thus wants to show that phantasy results from a being whose significance is both "real and never finished."[123] The intentions of the imaginary, he wants to say, are at bottom co-terminated in a real ontology, and thus we must understand the "symbolic matrix" of the imagination to take place within a "fecund imprint," that of the "reactivation and transformation of precedent institutions."[124]

One cannot intentionally call upon this hitherto unknown significance, for it is contained in the apparitional power that belongs to the phenomenon. Moreover, there is nothing we can do to fit this newly arising significance into an existing context. Significant events are instead indeterminate in what they offer in meaning. They thus must be distinguished from events that merely *trigger*, which take us out of our present and customary path, but do not themselves open up a new avenue. Significant events are, more profoundly, primal-institutions (*Urstiftung*), the validity of which is inseparably linked to a genesis of being that differs from a present context in such a way as to demand a new comportment. The significant event thus bears a novelty that breaks through in order to function as *index sui*, as an archetype that can thenceforward only be copied. Proust's *Recherche* (Search) can be regarded as the attempt to rediscover such events, starting with a present that stirs up resonance and reawakens the lost archetype. Merleau-Ponty finds in the writings of Proust a way to understand and recover a primal institution of the lost archetype in the desire to return to it. Proust treats objects as capable of an unveiling power, which opens up before the subject a meaning that is genative of both thing and desire of that thing.

Chapter 3

Proust and the Significant Event[1]

The work of art, for Lyotard, expresses what he calls the "deconciliation" between the structure of desire and the world of things. Artwork, Lyotard thinks, recovers a desire that transgresses temporality, and thus his treatment of the work of art depends on the notion that unconscious contents are fundamentally super-temporal. Indeed, it could be said that Freud allows for such a reading, especially when he discusses matters such as trauma, repression, forgetting, etc. In trauma, for example, past events are traumatogenic only afterwards, through some later scene that allows the past scene to be recalled. In this sense, trauma is made possible for Freud only on the basis of a simultaneity of temporal moments in which the past is not obliterated but generated by the present. Previous traumas are unforgettably traumatic in that the psyche constantly repeats them. For the psyche, "to be" is "traumatize-ing," its existence a ceaseless generation of the past that exists not because it *was* but because it is re-presented by the psyche in the now. Such a psyche owes its existence to a more general deconciliation between the times of a psychical desiring and an objectivity desired. This apparent non-relation between desiring and the desired object, we may also notice, can only occur because of a simultaneous forgetting of object in the unforgettability or repetition of desire. Here one can also speak of the deconciliation inherent to a repression of the desirable: repression for Freud requires a return of the repressed in such a way that the latter is desired but has been rendered tolerable only because it is hidden or forgotten in the desiring. The repressed is also something to which conscious life is deconciled in a second-order sense, therefore, because it is part of the psyche that we wish will remain impossible, unknown or unwanted, and thus for Freud it partakes in a death instinct that wishes for nothing more to remember – a sublime state of forgetting, as it were.

Merleau-Ponty shares with Freud the thesis of simultaneity between temporal moments. For both thinkers, there is a return of some repressed past into the present. This requires them both to say, too, that repression is a way of retaining the past by expressing (literally ex-pressing, pushing it outside) it – retaining the past precisely by getting rid of it in the now – inadvertently or unintentionally. The past-present inherent within expression is not only the expression of the forgotten or desired object but also of a past that is thought to be in some way alien to conscious life. But whereas Freud understands this internal alienation of the forgotten from present conscious life on the basis of the instinctive impulse of Negation, like that of the death instinct, and thus on the basis of a radical break or deconcilia-tion between desiring and the desired object, Merleau-Ponty under-stands both desiring and the desired object to betray an implicit temporality belonging within both terms. Thus, for him, the desired object invokes a return of a repressed or forgotten time that struc-tures the impulse towards it.

This chapter examines Merleau-Ponty's reading of the Proustian *Recherche* for a hidden and lost time into which the present desire attempts to return. Proust's search to retrieve a lost time, according to Merleau-Ponty, very explicitly deals with this structure of desire. Proustian nostalgia, for him, is on a search not merely to generate the past event in the now and only in the now, but rather to reclaim the being of the past event, that is, to animate the past anew and with all of its original significance and sense apart from active remember-ing. The search for a lost time is not helped by activity or perfor-mance in which I am responsible for articulating the past in quite particular ways – it is not, in this sense, merely reminiscence – but the hope for the past to unfold itself and come forth out of the dark back-ward abysm of time.[2]

Merleau-Ponty is apparently mindful of this possible ontological recursivity, and the return of its original significance, when he writes one of the densest Working Notes of *The Visible and the Invisible*. Titled "Indestructible past, and intentional analytic – and ontology," the note is as follows:

The Freudian idea of the unconsciousness and the past as "inde-structible," as "intemporal" = elimination of the common idea of time as a "series of *Erlebnisse*" – There is an architectonic past, c.f. Proust: the *true* hawthorns are the hawthorns of the past – Restore this life without *Erlebnisse*, without interiority . . . which is, in reality, the "monumental" life, *Stiftung*, initiation.

This "past" belongs to a mythical time, to the time before time, to the prior life . . . [3]

An architectonic past here refers to a past understood from the perspective of a monumental and initiating being or *Stiftung*. It is thus a past, according to Merleau-Ponty, which links into the present and future in such a way that allows the discrete moments to flow into one another on the basis of a succession and which is generative of a meaning on the basis of this succession. The otherwise separated moments, insofar as they precede or proceed through one another, come to be meaningful only against the background of this architectonic principle. Thus the significance of these moments is in fact the result of a primal-institution or architectonic past and is thus inseparable from genesis. In this sense the meaning of an event is always indeterminate since it bears a significance that is in constant change. Yet, in another sense, there is no meaning without this significance since meaning here only ever arises on its basis. Proust's search in the present to overcome forgetting is thus a search for the original event from out of which significance first arises. It is a search for a significance from out of which the various possible meanings of things arise. Proust's search for the past, according to Merleau-Ponty, inevitably becomes a search for the architectonic past and thus for the being that institutes the present. Elsewhere, Merleau-Ponty again links the notion of *Stiftung* with remembrances, as when he says that the foundational being of consciousness requires a "noble forgetting" of the entire range of significance for the present and "continue[s] to have value after their appearance."[4] In "the unlimited fecundity of each present," he adds, these past events "perpetually come to life again."[5] In a certain sense, one could understand Proust's search for a lost, architectonic time as a search to discover the unlimited fecundity of each present since it is an attempt to retrieve the original significant event from out of the present.

Merleau-Ponty's rendering of Proustian forgetting, which appeals to the forgotten architectonic past, allows him to explain the restoration of the past event in the present phenomenon in such a way that points back to an unlimited fecundity or continually instituting principle underneath what is now being offered to meaning. Here Merleau-Ponty can reiterate that the return of the past into the present ultimately undoes the assumption that we simply recall the past. For, in the sense that bringing something into presence or allowing something to fall into oblivion (memory) is in fact more about an event in being than it is about an activity, memory is implicitly born of an inadvertent ontological recursivity. To forget and to remember thus ultimately have "the fundamental structure of *Zeitigung*."[6] They belong, more profoundly, to what Merleau-Ponty calls in another Working Note an "Existential eternity" that "transcend[s] the past present distinction," in order to retain an "*Ineinander*," the "enveloping-enveloped" of the present-past.[7] Memorial dimensions thus owe their existence to a deeper region of being. They are, in fact, localizations of an "*Urstiftung* of a point in time."[8]

One could say that, rather than a property of an active consciousness, the dimensions of the memorial thus *come over* the subject and that memory is in fact the result of subjection. This leads us to think that the search for a time past, insofar as it is not in fact an endless quest to retain merely a past point in time, may in fact be achieved not by willing but by comporting oneself to the manner of being in which an actual recurrence of the forgotten is possible. In his essay "The Image of Proust," for instance, Walter Benjamin writes of the Proustian, "Penelope work of recollection," the woof to the warp of forgetting.[9] For Merleau-Ponty, too, the dynamic between the forgotten and the recalled allows for optimism within the tragedy of having lost the past. At the same time that there is a departure from this forgotten and lost time of the past event, the now forgotten event also contains the possibility of returning to it. Merleau-Ponty's intentional analytic in the above Working Note is in a certain sense the carrying out of an implicitly Proustian hope to return to the forgotten past. Perhaps it is precisely this internal hope within the Proustian nostalgic impulse that allows Merleau-Ponty to speak of the simultaneity between the architectonic and mythical times in order to describe the way in which we gain access into the ontological recursivity inherent within the present phenomenon.

Architectonic time and myth time: these times guide Merleau-Ponty's reflections on Proust in the above Note. First, there is an architectonic time, the time of an archetypal past. On the basis of this time there is a nostalgic impulse and desire to return to the past time from which the present time inherits its present meaning. The architectonic time is thus a significant time. This significance, Merleau-Ponty wants to say, already bears a mythico-poetic quality that one must let reassert itself on its own terms, that is, let it show without actively willing it to come about, in order to reveal anew its "prior life" of the "time before time." It is thus necessary to see the architectonic time and the mythic time, for Merleau-Ponty in his treatment of Proust, not as two separated times. The belonging-together of these timings, I want to say here, ultimately refers to the institution that both allows things to mean for us as well as to be drawn near to those things. The belonging-together of the architectonic and myth times, insofar as they function on the basis of a simultaneous principle of institution, reveals for Merleau-Ponty both the original significant event as well as the way in which the event can be finally recuperated precisely as the original significant event.

Proust discovers the latter, mythic time through the literary work of art itself. Thus the literary work does not originate for Proust out of an active recollection of the past but rather it comes to be from out of the original and significant architectonic past. The radicality of the literary work of art, I will say towards the end of this chapter, complicates the notion of text as that which renders the unclarity of an image in fixed terms. The text of the literary work, for Proust, is thus not different than an image, especially as it was understood in the last chapter by Merleau-Ponty, insofar as it is nothing less than the revelation of the principle institution that is both in the symbolic functioning of things as well as the desire and the compellation towards those things.

Architectonic Time

Though desire endlessly seeks to express itself, this recursion does not imply for Proust that it is structured on the basis of an original negation.

Nor does it imply that the past object that structures this desire can be found in a past point in time. The past, for Proust, is happening in the now not because desire is structured by any kind of negation but because it is structured and initiated by the evocative power inherent to chance encounters with objects in the present. This power of evocation brings the recursive structure of desire into relation with meaning in the present object that is generated by the lost time of an originary event. Consider, for example, Proust's famous passage on tasting a *petite madeleine* dipped in tea:

> And as soon as I had recognized the taste of the piece of madeleine dipped in lime-blossom tea that my aunt used to give me (though I did not yet know and had to put off to much later discovery why this memory made me so happy), immediately the old gray house on the street, where her bedroom was, came like a stage set to attach itself to the little wing opening onto the garden that had been built for my parents behind it (that truncated section which was all I had seen before then); and with the house the town, from morning to night and in all weathers, the Square, where they sent me before lunch, the streets where I went on errands, the paths we took if the weather was fine . . .[10]

Here the present taste sensation stimulates the recollection of the past taste sensation and hence the past occasion itself.[11] It is not a question of a mere external association between two distinct and discriminate sensations and events, since the two moments are not experienced as merely similar but identical. The past and present have been made to intrude on one another, and thus the ordinary experience of time as a series of separated "nows" is transformed to a perpetual recapturing and recalling of the past.[12] The *petite madeleine* evokes a hitherto unknown sense of temporality that it is not subject to the vicissitudes of ordinary temporal mutability but goes beyond the limits of such a time.[13]

The *mémoire involontaire* is in effect quite different than an intellectual memory. The latter is in a certain sense dead to the past. It distinguishes itself from a past event that it takes to be irretrievable and in fact unavailable to recollection.[14] The intellectual memory is in this sense voluntary and at our disposal insofar as it does not seek to achieve a living past.[15] Because it is invoked by a chance encounter with some significant object, and thus because it is not at all voluntary, the *mémoire involontaire* reveals to us another sort of past. This past, according to Proust, is given back to us in a livelier way. The *petite madeleine* releases a memory of something like an "aura" of the thing in which the thing also gives back a desirable set of relations associated with it from a time recalled. The *madeleine* brings about a past that is not absolutely irretrievable and not absolutely absent in remembrances. This is a past that rejuvenates itself, despite ourselves. It is not like a solitary atom, not one singular, localizable moment, which is incapable of evoking its own sense.[16] The traversal of time that the *mémoire involontaire* brings to life rests upon the fact that the mind itself has no role in recalling the past because it happens when the past has been completely forgotten, literally a "lost time."

In *The Phenomenology of Perception,* Merleau-Ponty explicitly links Proustian remembrances to a phenomenological time in which, "[m]y present outruns itself in the direction of an immediate future and an immediate past and impinges upon them where they actually are, namely, in the past and in the future themselves."[17] Intentionality is shown not to unravel linearly but to occur on the basis of a double movement of protention and retention. I cannot say that one perception begins, continues or stops without calling into question the matter of implicit phases. Such an experience is not itself retained in the field of presence but rather overflows it. For, in the movement of one perception to another I at least implicitly make reference to the primordial character of succession underlying two distinct phenomena in which there is already a promise of repetition. This subtending succession or running-off of the present into the not-present recalls the "operative intentionality" of Husserlian time-consciousness, the aim of which is to problematize the theme of a perfect given of the thing so that it no longer appears in phenomenology as an external limit but as a primary-remembering and awakening and as forward-directing. This consequent imperfection and limitedness denies a cancelling out of the mystery and depth by the present phenomenon and the subject who is the ultimate source of that appearance. In phenomenological time, there is also the possibility within the present

phenomenon that the subject may be disrupted or surprised by the
as yet unforeseen appearing.

In the sense that *The Visible and the Invisible* problematizes intentional constitution as the absolute source of meaning, and in turn
expands on a thesis of *Zeitloss* that we find mentioned in the chapter
on "Temporality" in *Phenomenology of Perception* – the possibility for the
surprising un-presented moment to invade into the present so that
one may be overwhelmed by the loss of time itself – the writings
of Proust no longer serve to explain explicit givenness for Merleau-
Ponty so much as they elucidate what is dormant within that givenness.
The potential recursion of time is extended to include a more explicit
thesis of auto-constitution that subjugates the consciousness of acts
and decisions.[18] The radicalization in *The Visible and the Invisible* can
be taken to have an especially Proustian bent, for the traversal of time
in the *mémoire involontaire* operates only inasmuch as the lost place
announces or generates itself in the present phenomenon. When
Proust refers to the coincidence of temporal moments, according to
Merleau-Ponty, he refers to something that is really "behind the sensible" or even "in its heart."[19] He thus describes, "a new type of being,
a being by porosity, pregnancy, or generality and he before whom the
horizon opens is caught up, included within it."[20]

We might say, then, that a present recollection allows the forgotten
event to unfold or articulate itself. This articulation is not per se a *re-
enactment* of the past so much as it is one announcement of the past
event's initial indetermination. In this sense memory is allowed to
move back and forth between present and past because of an incoherence with which the initial physical event was already pregnant. It
is the "physical voluptuousness" of the initial event, Melreau-Ponty
writes in a direct quote from Proust, with which the "inward domain
is diversified and adorned."[21] The physical site of the original event
contains the possible meanings of how it will announce itself in memory, so that we might say there is a drive to memory outside of itself
and because of which memory seeks to reassemble the past. Memory
is thus externalized and is in fact a form of what Merleau-Ponty calls
the "perpetual enterprise of taking our bearings on the constellations of the world" and the those "things on our dimensions."[22]

The last pages of *The Visible and the Invisible*, in which Merleau-Ponty pays special attention to the chapter "Swann in Love" in *Swann's Way*, reveals the memorial enterprise of ceaselessly recovering a meaning from out of the original event. "Swann in Love" contains the passages that have caused many a reader to drown along with Swann in the sway of his passions, and Merleau-Ponty is perhaps no different. He is especially caught by the fine sequence in which one evening at a dinner party Swann hears Vintieul's Sonata and the "little phrases" of the violinist. These phrases are at first to Swann a "liquid rippling of sound, multiform," "pleasing," "enrapturing" and "exquisite," "slender and robust."[23] But in a certain sense they become, by increments, far more than this. Their impression, writes Proust, "would continue to envelop in its liquidity, its ceaseless overlapping, the motifs which from time to time emerge."[24]

The deep impression of the little phrases themselves, the meaning of which recurs in different ways over and over again for Swann, implies that the phrases constantly activate new meanings in order to announce themselves in the present. They thus do not have any fixed meaning. Proust in fact writes that the little phrases of the sonata are not initially "design," "architecture" or "thought." In fact, it is their lack of fixity that gives the phrases their ability to open up to Swann a new series of meanings. The present meaning becomes nothing less than the exposure of a possible meaning that was contained in the deep impression of the little phrases.

Yet Merleau-Ponty also writes of the little phrases: "Each time we want to get at it immediately or lay hands on it, or circumscribe it, or see it unveiled, we do in fact feel that the attempt is misconceived, that it retreats in the measure that we approach."[25] As much as they open up a new sense in the present, that is, the lost things thus also contain another past sense that is in perpetual retreat.[26] Some original aspect of the violinist's little phrases must absent itself at the same time another of its aspects is called up. The phrases involve a constant negotiation between the present meaning and the past event. But it is not immediately clear how the original event of the phrases provide space for new meanings, or how new meanings are just re-articulations of the phrases. Merleau-Ponty hints that the phrases contain or even are "the essence of love."[27] He is referring here to the reciprocity between the little phrases from Vinteuil and Swann's growing affections for his lover, Odette. When first he meets her, Odette strikes Swann, "not, certainly, as being devoid of beauty, but as endowed with a kind of beauty which left him indifferent, which aroused in him no desire."[28] But immediately after hearing the little phrases and then spotting Odette passing by on the street, without yet knowing who she was, Swann experienced her as though she were herself the violin sonata. Proust writes that the phrases inevitably become a "national anthem" for his growing affections.[29] This begins to seal Swann's love for Odette, as later does the fact that Swann is struck by Odette's "resemblance to the figure Zipporah, Jethro's daughter in a fresco of the Sistine Chapel."[30]

There is the feeling that the previously shallow Odette has been supplied with the depths of the sonata itself. The little phrases are endowed from the beginning with an ability to be revived time and again, but each time they are a new meaning is brought out from them: first exquisite and robust, they are later able to stand in the place of Swann's love for Odette. This of course will speak to something essentially tragic in Swann and Odette's love affair, and in the very last phrases "Swann in Love" Swann laments, "To think that I've wasted years of my life, that I've longed to die, that I've experienced my greatest love, for a woman who didn't appeal to me, who wasn't even my type!"[31] Yet the reservoir also betrays a significance inherent to the little phrases themselves such that they may be recalled differently and in different ways. In this sense the little phrases are central to Merleau-Ponty's considerations of Proust since they function as the first event that will bear the significance of Swann and Odette's love affair and thus the various meanings the affair will come to take on.

It is thus important to Merleau-Ponty that the phrases themselves do fall back and become forgotten precisely when they are recalled in some manner. What is remembered does not stand in discord with what is forgotten, but each time Swann recalls the little phrases again something different about them is exaggerated and something else is left behind. Though we cannot say here that in the *mémoire involontaire* we find an actual, or factual, constitution of the past, it is also not true that the *mémoire involontaire* highlights a fundamental non-identity between a self and the self who the former attempts to recapture by recapturing a past time. The importance of the *mémoire involontaire* is that both the original event and present, as well as their meanings in relation to one another, occur on the basis of a temporal succession that links them to one another. They thus require a principle of significance more basic than each term. This significance is explained by Merleau-Ponty on the basis of what he calls in the Working Note above an architectonic being that is forever instituting itself in the present.

I should point out, too, that at the same time the architectonic being and the significance that arises on its basis provides the possibility for the so-called Penelope work of memory. But, insofar as it is not more than the succession of time itself, this architectonic structure also frustrates memory since it cannot ever be entirely captured or reconstructed. It is nevertheless important that this being conveys the possibility of memorialization for Merleau-Ponty precisely because it resists the categories of a metaphysical time, and it is this resistance that allows Merleau-Ponty, in his reading of Proust, to bring seeming opposites of remembering and forgetting together and to expose their "underlying bond"[32] that gives sustenance to memory in the first place.

Myth Time

Time says, Walter Beimel, is the main character of *Remembrance of Things Past*.[33] The book is about a lost time in particular, for it is this lost time that endures throughout the work, unended by the present scene and containing the potential for all other times. The book, a tome dedicated to a meditation on the memorial, shows that the past time after which memory seeks is not grasped by a psychical return to the same. The memorial, for Proust, is constituted by an original event in time. The significance of this event for the present is understood on the basis of a succession. The memorial thus implicitly requires a multitude of points of view insofar as it is at once both present and lost within the things past. It implies what Beimel calls a "polyperspectivity" in which the differentiation between temporal moments is inserted into one's inner life. Kristeva also points out in *Proust and the Sense of Time* that Proustian temporality, "cuts through the categories of metaphysics, bringing together opposites like idea, duration and space on the one hand, and force, perception, limitation and desire on the other."[34] Since "bringing things together is a metaphor,"[35] we may also say that Proustian temporality is a metaphorical temporality that brings a so-called interiority of consciousness into connection with its exterior.

A metaphorical time – the time that bridges oppositions – is understood not on the basis of pre-established dates but rather eras, aeons, epochs, episodes, and narratives through which temporal moments can be strung together.[36] It is myth time, then, the time of eras, aeons, episodes, narratives, etc., which will give an account of the sudden upraising of the abysm in the visible that may at any time surprise the subject and subjective constitution and expose the ultimate falsity a wholly theoretical interiority. For myth operates on the basis of a time that not only remains close to and crosses into the architectonic and significant event but can bring this primacy into a not-yet theoretical language precisely only because the time of this architectonic event is itself metaphorical. Myth and architectonic time thus refer to a unified temporality, but still the former aspect will be the expression of a wish to capture the initial metaphoricity of significant event. It is a form of language in which the metaphoricity of significance remains as such, undisturbed, and yet gains a certain insight into this significance in order to bring it into expression.

In a comment on the relationship between philosophy and literature in *The Visible and the Invisible*, Merleau-Ponty again refers to the paradox of expression, this time in connection to the myth time of significant events: "expression of the mute experience by itself," which "is creation," is a,

> creation that is at the same time a reintegration of being: for it is not a creation in the sense of one of the commonplace *Gebilde* that history fabricates: it knows itself to be *Gebilde* and wishes to surpass itself as *pure Gebilde*, to find again its origin. It is hence a creation in a radical sense: a creation that is at the same time an adequation, the only way to obtain an adequation.[37]

In surpassing itself as pure construction or structure, the literary work is a turning back on itself. It knows itself as construction and, in showing itself thus, at the same time hopes to recuperate the originary significance of the object-field upon which it is constructed. Precisely in giving itself *as a construction*, we may say, literature reaches back (in the suggestive sense of *zurückfragen*, i.e., literally "asks back for") towards that which has offered itself for this construction. Merleau-Ponty thus resists the claim that the fictitious is arbitrarily compounded, and out of touch with the factical. In *Ideas I*, Husserl had already linked with *Dichtung* and *Phantasieren*, even acknowledging that the former is dependent on the latter, and thus he was aware that the literary work might exceed phenomenology because of its facilities of description and imaginative variation of the contingent fact. Phenomenology, even for Husserl, discovers a phantasy that is not itself mere empirical description at the same time that it alters an otherwise obstinate desire for purity in the eidetic. We can never derive the essence of a fact, Husserl discovers, without the help of phantasy.[38]

Merleau-Ponty wants to say with Husserl that the intelligibility of empirical facts (such as historical facts) is inseparable from phantastical constructions (such as in literature). The literary work addresses itself to the various meanings in a field of objects, even when it is clearly not engaged with the objects of fact. In "Metaphysics and the Novel," Merleau-Ponty goes so far as to argue that literature is inherently endowed with metaphysical power of penetration not in the classic sense that it refers "to God, to Consciousness," nor in the sense that it escapes into a world and "attain[s] a perfect transparence" but in the sense that it describes the "hybrid modes of expression," the "loves" and "hates" that are "a contact with the world which precedes all thought *about* the world."[39] Here he attempts to go beyond Husserl's *Ideas I* on the basis of an implicit oneiric character in the world. It is not merely that *Dichtung* is dependent on *Phantasieren* for Merleau-Ponty but also that this phantasy is just as concerned as phenomenology with grasping meanings and that it displays the same desire to seize and penetrate into them as they appear into visibility. Since the work turns to the field-structure of objects, it accepts to descend into the most profound and abysmal depths where the imaginary then

allows itself the possibility to encounter the real in its most illicit and
compelling figurations. The literary work, according to Merleau-Ponty,
cannot settle into a supposedly intangible alterior space of fiction
apart from phenomenology, since the imaginary upon which it is
based is itself an openness to remain within the life of the phenomenon, prior to the founding abstraction that conceals the formation of
meaning.

The movement in "Swann's Way" from hearing the violinist's little
phrases to Swann's falling in love implies a series of metaphors, "overprintings," an "imaginary journeying from metaphor to metaphor"
which "both irradiate and contaminate each other," and "chain the
meaning of one another."[40] It is sometimes even argued that Proustian
metaphor operates only inasmuch as it is supported by metonymy,
and that it is in fact the latter that opens the way for metaphoric
possibilities.[41] The succession of metaphors induced by the initial
encounter with the little phrases is thus made possible by an underlying nexus of juxtapositions and associations that are always already
inherent within what Proust describes as the "robust" and "tumultuous"
phrases themselves. This is what apparently catches Merleau-Ponty's
attention when he writes that the little phrases "open vortexes in the
sonorous world" that "finally form one sole vortex in which the ideas
fit in with one another."[42]

The literary work of art, for Proust, purposefully opens up an original significance from out of which all possible meanings arise. It does
so, however, precisely by showing how the newly arisen meaning is
indeterminate. The Search in particular, for Proust, hopes to display
the significant event that gives rise to various meaning formations
and the potential for indeterminate and multiple meanings. Proust's
novel is in this way meta-literature. Its *modus operandi* is to use objects
as signifying events that indicate a world's structure of referential
totalities.[43] The work's genius is that it shows a world not graspable
prior to our encounter with things, a world that does not function as
an essence and is not a unifying ideality that introduces some perfect
mean behind things, but rather a world obtained through a slanting
ray of sun, an odour, a flavour, a draft, etc., which may at first appear to
give us merely subjective associations but in fact proliferate and finally
move in the direction of a series of referential totalities. The world

conveyed by Proust is in this sense always still to be made, always under revision, always already proliferating, multiplying and defying the quotidian logic of appearances.[44]

It is sometimes remarked that the very fragility of Proust's search for a time past is itself born from the hope to disclose a bond in the otherwise dissatisfied and fragmentary life of the work's narrator (Proust himself). The work he creates reveals that the present object, which appears to us on the basis of various associations that continually proliferate such that its precise meaning always remains unsettled, has a significance from out of which this indeterminacy arises. The present thing, in order to bear significance, thus arises insofar as it does not merely partake in a linear series but is subtended by a more basic principle of temporal relation. The thing's significance is in this sense determined only insofar as it is an event in time and where this time contains the possibility of new meanings to emerge from out of it. What *is* said of this present event thus allows a meaning contained in the past event to come into view or to emerge. What *will be* said of this present event allows yet another meaning contained in the past event to come into view. These two newly arising meanings from out of the past event do not highlight two exclusive and separate meanings of the past. They highlight, rather, a significance that always already contains a complex or mesh of meanings.

In *The Visible and the Invisible*, Merleau-Ponty thus links Proustian significance to an "amorphous world of experience" which "nevertheless evokes and provokes everything in general" and "is at bottom Being in Heidegger's sense, which . . . appears as containing everything that will ever be said, and yet leaving us to create it (Proust)."[45] The significance of the thing, the thing about which we can say or even can "will to say" (*vouloir-dire*) anything, emerges from out of a being that thus contains everything that is "to be said" (*quelque chose à dire*) but nevertheless does not dictate in what way it is in fact said.[46] Merleau-Ponty repeats something like this in *The Phenomenology of Perception* when he cites a passage from *Remembrance* in which Proust writes of the "inner book" of experience that, "speech and writing mean to *translate* . . . into a text by the word experience itself calls forth."[47] The inner book of experience is just the claim that explicitly given objects implicitly open up into a successive relation that is underneath them, and that this experience itself operates like a text. It is something to be read, interpreted, explained etc. Walter Benjamin points out in "The Image of Proust" that "*textum* means 'web'" and that the text itself is the "*actus purus* of recollection itself," while "author and plot is only the reverse of the continuum of memory, the pattern on the back side of the tapestry."[48]

The very format of Proust's work – it is a novel, yes, but also an extensive memoire complete with historical facts and even on occasion fabulations about historical events – tells of the literary work's indebtedness to this basic field-structure of objects. The literary work of art, for Proust, is imaginary journeyings or overprintings of image upon image precisely in order to call upon this fundamental *textum* that is already implicit in things and on the basis of which things are given their significance to us. There is ultimately no cure for the nostalgic impulse, in fact, except through the literary work that respects the reality of particularity and multiplicity in order to grasp not merely the real but the metaphoricity that is prior to the real.

Text and Image

There is a hidden *textum* of objects, for Proust, such that they occur against a more fundamental grounding that allows them to relate to one another in a significant way. Merleau-Ponty discovers in the painting, too, a polysemy that implicates not merely the external face of the thing but its complex, its indeterminate significance in what it offers to meaning. Proust thus allows us to see the text's relation to this latent indeterminacy and to see the text as a participant in the same task of the image. Roland Barthes says that the text functions to "fix" this dysfunction of the image, that the text is "a way to counter the terror of uncertain signs," since it "helps to identify . . . the elements of the scene and the scene itself." Whereas the meaning of the image is always unfinished, he says, the text exists as "an anchorage of all possible (denoted) meaning of the object . . ."[49] It is precisely this messianic aspect of the text that Proustian time complicates.

This complication of the relation between text and image in Proust's writings, however, requires that we first recognize, following

Merleau-Ponty's treatment, the way in which he returns language in general to the indeterminate significant event when he equates language with the little phrases of the violinist:

> Why not admit – what Proust knew very well and said in another place – that language as well as music can sustain a sense of virtue of its own arrangement, catch a meaning in its own mesh, that it does so without exception each time it is conquering, active, creative language, each time something is, in the strong sense, said? Why not admit that, just as the musical notation is a facsimile made after the event, an abstract portrait of the musical entity, language as a system of explicit relations between signs and signified, sounds and meaning, is a product of the operative language in which sense and sound are in the same relationship as the "little phrases" and the five notes in it afterwards?[50]

Here Proust gives Merleau-Ponty the means to launch a more radical critique of a language-system in Saussure's sense than in "Indirect Language and the Voices of Silence." A language-system, for Saussure, is the heterogeneous and systematic totality with which the linguist is initially faced and which may be studied from a variety of points of view (the physical, the physiological, the mental, the individual and the social), and Merleau-Ponty initially sought to remove the heterogeneity of this language-system by understanding it on the basis of the so-called mute science of painting. But now, at least in a certain sense, there is a shift from understanding the otherwise heterogeneous system of language on the basis of the mute or indirect logic of painting. Language does not stand out from a mute background but rather is itself a kind of mute art, and a direct participant in hitherto unexpressed meanings. The silence of being is in this sense already a language, already something for language or already on the way to language.

I want to say that, in service of this treatment of language, the text of the literary work of art, for Proust, cannot in fact counter the so-called terror of uncertainty in the image so much as it brings that very uncertainty into existence. The text thus elaborates a double function for Proust: there is the text of the book that serves to confer the sequences of images, the imaginary journeyings or overprintings, from the original event onwards; but this highlights that, for Proust, the text of the literary work is itself an image insofar as it renders the indeterminate itself. Blanchot says that, in Proust's works, the "transformation of time into an imaginary space" implies that "there is no more interiority, for everything that is interior is deployed outwardly."[51] The pages of the literary work of art, for Blanchot, confer the intimate "entirely outside" such that the page itself becomes "more inaccessible and more mysterious than the innermost thought."[52] This is the same relation between apparently opposing terms that Merleau-Ponty, following Paul Valéry, describes as "the secret blackness of milk" that is "only accessible through its whiteness".[53]

For Proust, and for Merleau-Ponty reading Proust, the text of the literary work of art not only struggles against an explicit meaning in order to retain the indeterminate; it also functions to reveal how the author is himself dispossessed and unended since he is only discoverable through the text. This relation between text and author thus conveys a duplicity that could be understood, in part, through a libido-theory for which the origin of meaning does not depend on explicit textual interplay but rather on the operation of an energetic activity upon sign-structures. The text of the literary work of art reveals that there is a significative rupture introduced into each sign-system only by means of a pulsating movement that is itself indetermined, and it is here that we can locate, outside in the world, what is most intimate of the author himself.

Proust does not follow Freud's claim that writing expresses "unsatisfied wishes" and lays bare the "motive force of phantasies" in order to serve as a "correction of unsatisfying reality."[54] It is true, however, that any thing in Proust's writings can function as a sign for phantasy and consequently as a sign for an apparent specificity different from other possible worlds overlaying the site of the event where it was first grasped. But Proust does not take the specificity of this phantastical world to reveal a satisfying principle of desire that gives aesthetic pleasure *set against* an unsatisfying principle of reality. The text of the literary work, for Proust, in fact betrays a desire that originates from out of an original encounter. It maps the present enjoyment or pleasure in a thing back into some primal encounter of which the entire meaning was not previously determined. The text, which fills the

book and really does draw out the link between the present enjoyment and a primal event, is thus able to confer the original field-
structure of things. Here the literary work of art aims to regain not
the past time but an original significance underneath things. It conveys a significant event that generates both the present meaning of
a thing as well as the compulsion to regain the event along with its
significance.

The text of the literary work of art, from its beginning to end, thus
defies what Merleau-Ponty calls in the April 1961 Working Note a
"series of *Erlebnisse*." It is the expression of a meaning that has not
been grasped through an act of sense. The text conveys a grasping of
meaning that follows a direction and takes a path towards the original event and into the multi-various meanings that is always already
implicit in the event itself. In the lecture titled "Institution in Personal
and Public History," Merleau-Ponty thus characterizes Proust's search
as "an indefinite elaboration" of an event that is "continually under
revision."[55] We could say, borrowing from Merleau-Ponty, that the
text finally allows us to "leave the philosophy of *Erlebnisse*," allows us to
leave the categories of the thing, the thing as it is meant, and the act
of sense that grasps this meaning, in order to once and for all see the
significance that grounds these categories and contains the basis for
each term, that is, to "pass into the philosophy of our *Urstiftung*."[56]

The True Hawthorns are the Hawthorns of the Past

Merleau-Ponty writes in the passage quoted at the beginning of this
chapter, "the true hawthorns are the hawthorns of the past." This is a
reference to Swann's childhood ecstasies over the hawthorn path
"throbbing with their fragrance," which he sadly leaves behind one
day for Paris:

> "Oh, my poor little hawthorns," I was assuring them through my
> sobs, "it isn't you who want to make me unhappy, to force me to
> leave you. You, you've never done me any harm. So I shall always
> love you." And, drying my eyes, I promised them that, when I grew
> up, I would never copy the foolish example of other men, but

that even in Paris, on fine spring days, instead of paying calls and
listening to silky talk, I would set off for the country to see the first
hawthorn-trees in bloom.[57]

The hawthorns of the past to which Swann wishes to continually
return are not for Merleau-Ponty merely "reverberations" of the past,
the past again coming upon Swann and re-striking him.[58] The possible movement between present to past is more enduring: "the past,"
Merleau-Ponty writes of Proust, "takes on the outline of a preparation
or premeditation of a present that exceeds it in meaning although
it recognizes itself in it."[59] In an important sense, Swann's mistake is
that each spring he will actually return to the hawthorns of Combray.
This is the same mistake that he makes in his supposed love for Odette,
according to Merleau-Ponty. Love for Swann never goes beyond
"habit, since it involves a transference of a way of loving learned elsewhere or in childhood."[60] But such a love, Merleau-Ponty continues,
is not more than an "interior image of the object" and really not "ever
lived by anyone."[61] What Swann continually fails to see is that his form
of love involves a "pure negation" of the present, which makes it
"impossible."[62] What he cannot ever bring himself to do is to bring
back the *true* past, not the impossible past but the past that is the "fact
of negation," in which the present hawthorn contains, as a lining or
depth, the hawthorns of his childhood home.[63] We might say that
Swann cannot really retrieve the pastness of the past hawthorn simply
by returning to its semblance in Combray. But this is not to say that
for Proust our present does not continually force us, involuntarily, to
be comported to the past. There is a pastness always already opera-
tional in the hawthorn.

Swann's failure to see this tacit form of comportment towards
the past demands an obvious question: How then do we comport
ourselves to the past without recourse to semblance? In the literary
work of art, Merleau-Ponty says, "Proust envisages a *via negativa* of
love."[64] Such a love is not what Swann achieves for himself, but it is
nevertheless what the book achieves since it aims to exceed the
explicit meaning of the present thing in order to retrieve a past
significance in the present. Ultimately, then, the Penelope work of
memory is achieved only by the work that takes its project not merely

to superimpose the image upon the object but rather to revert into the temporality of the object itself in order to grasp it through its series of relations. The work thus addresses itself to things in the form of a myth time that allows the original event to endure into the present without needing to fix or anchor it.

Remembrance of Things Past never forgets that its work, to find its way back to the lost time of the event, and thus to assuage the nostalgic impulse, cannot simply ruminate on memories reflexively. One must speak of memories the way that memories speak. Thus the literary work of art does not *create* memory but it endlessly searches through the sequence of images already contained in memory in order give a viewpoint that is valid for all. The literary work of art finally functions to render explicit what Dillon describes as "carnal knowing" that takes the author beyond mere romance and into a genuine intimacy because here he has the ability to genuinely sense the other's sensing of himself.[65] The book itself ultimately reminds us of Proust's oft-repeated saying that love is time made tangible.

Chapter 4

A Figurative Dimension:
Reversibility Between the Arts

Merleau-Ponty writes in "Eye and Mind" that "[i]t is Matisse who taught us to see . . . contours not in a "physical-optical" way but rather as structural filaments, as the axes of a corporeal system of activity and passivity." Matisse, according to Merleau-Ponty, helps us see not the outward shape of things, nor the diagrammatical scheme of those things. There are no indissoluble unities in the Matisse painting, nor do things vary in terms of possible propositions. Each line of the canvas rather undermines the measure of things, allowing things to be shown as they unfold from out of a region that is prior to objectivity and to the painter. Thus the line of a Matisse canvas is not more than a "structural filament," which follows back into this primal region and which, if it has a value, its value is "figurative." Here "the line is no longer a thing or an imitation of a thing. It is a certain disequilibrium kept up." It is the "restriction, segregation, or modulation of a pre-given spatiality."[1] Finally, according to Merleau-Ponty, it is Matisse who can thus teach us to see the figurative on the basis of a spatial region, prior to the human, from out of which things become things.

The line of the painting, for Matisse, is thus not simply representational. The thing conveyed by the painted line, to use the phraseology introduced in the opening passages of *The Visible and the Invisible*, is not simply there "at the end of my gaze [*regard*]" or "at the end of my exploration."[2] To paint or draw a line for Matisse is not simply to set the gaze against the thing, as the effect may be set against its cause. Rather, the painted line confers onto the canvas what Merleau-Ponty calls the "fragile act of the look [*regardant*]."[3] This subtle difference between gazing and looking , between an abstracted seeing and a concrete one, implies for Merleau-Ponty a passage from the "physical-optical" way of vision in which we see only "monocular images"[4] to a "binocular perception."[5] In the former, "the appearances are instantaneously stripped of a value"[6] and remain neutralized. Whereas in the latter, and in its return to the incarnated and stereo-scopic vision of two eyes, it is as if the "vision of world itself were formed from a certain point of the world."[7] This looking, looking from within a world, indeed "awakening to the world" so that "we cannot witness it as spectators,"[8] this is what Matisse seeks in the line.

He is in pursuit, then, of that inner fragility of looking, the hidden point at which the incarnated vision of his two eyes is laid open to the world in which it is inscribed. But this conferral of incarnated vision is doubly fragile, it seems, since as soon as there are eyes that look their movements "make the world vibrate – as one rocks a dolmen with one's finger without disturbing its fundamental solidity."[9] To convey the fragile act of the look requires that the painter must capture precisely that point of tension in incarnated vision where a newly awakening phenomenality also at the same time keeps something within it that is unmoved and alien to this vision, "as though the access to the world were but the other face of a withdrawal and this retreat to the margin of the world a servitude and another expression of my natural power to enter into it."[10] Finally, the fragility of looking is thereby conveyed by Matisse's figurative lines, those lines which aim not only to enter into the instability of the visible thing that has arisen from out of an alterity but also to render explicit this alterity as that which is behind perception. The figurative line is in this sense, according to Merleau-Ponty, not of things but of "floating pre-things."[11]

But what is the *figurative*, exactly? Though the figurative is part of a mimetology for Merleau-Ponty (partaking in the larger polyvalent lexicon, as in his repeated references to the imaginary, the fictive, the mythic, etc.), he is clear that it does not negate or nihilate an original object understood apart from artwork, only to be re-created by the work. In fact, the figurative originates from outside of itself. Merleau-Ponty thereby emphasizes what he calls a "figured philosophy" of the artwork, which restores an original "labour of vision" and the look that travels "an open circuit [that goes] from seeing body to visible body."[12] Merleau-Ponty's basic insight here is that the figurative ultimately betrays a vision that is forever *en route* between the body that

sees and the body that is seen. By figurative, then, he means to refer
to a more basic structuration of human existence that puts into play
a "seeing," "being seen" and "letting oneself be seen" all at once. The
figurative thus, more generally, bears an active form, a passive form
as well as an intermediary form. It participates in a circuit in order
to announce the "seeing-visible" of the body that is opened up by an
alterior looking upon the body.[13]

The active seer is thereby held out into a threshold over which it
cannot cross – what Merleau-Ponty calls the invisible of the world –
that usurps the activity of seeing and reveals itself as beyond the econ-
omy of natural life. At the same time that this invisibility manifests
itself, it thus also suspends the dogma of a wholly thematic consciousness. It should also be recalled from chapter two that, in relation to
this movement of one's self out into the alien, this open circuit is the
structure of what Merleau-Ponty calls desire. Thus, what the figures
of the artwork ultimately let us see is the various vicissitudes of desire.
One could say here that the figurative shows desire *in its desiring*. For
the artwork's figurations let us see desire as it travels its formative
path, as it arises in the site of one's body, travels outside of itself in
order to find satisfaction in the fullness of invisibility's presence, and
finally turns back on itself so that it can pass through the surface of
the body from whence it was originally incited.[14]

Here Merleau-Ponty acknowledges that, insofar as the figurative
nature of the artwork conveys the fragility of the look, and thus also
the very structure of desire through which this look is opened and
given its fragility, the work of art ultimately brings into play a site of
tactility, specifically a hand and a gesture that is fundamentally expressive of something more than itself. Not only is it through the gesture
that the artist moves beyond active "seeing" and into the passive
region of "being seen" or the "seeing-visible" of the body, but this
passive region is also the very place in which the artist is laid open to
invisibility precisely in order to bring it into visibility. The figured
work of art, it could be said, is not created *sui generis* so much as it is
brought about by that which has yet to be formed and is outside of or
apart from the gesture, and yet compelling the gesture into figuring
it. In this sense the figured artwork, through the gesture, is a surfeit
of determinations brought into a kind of relief. The work inevitably

calls to mind a specific sense of mimesis that traces back to the Latin *fingere* and even further to its Greek equivalent, *plassein/plattein*, which means "to figure" in the sense of "to fashion," "to model," or "to sculpt."

The figurative thereby betrays a mimetic stratification in Merleau-Ponty's thought: the figured work of art confers into existence a hidden texture and unthematic meaning underneath things as well as a compulsion that is derived from out of this texture. The figurations in this sense make apparent an erotic displacement. For the artist first moves out into this invisibility and only then relieves it by figuring it into a specific visibility. This specific relief is limited, since it functions by preserving some hitherto unexpressed and possible other figurations. The actually figured lines, in their connection with this open-ended relief, are finally made possible by a principle of reversibility that at once supports both the lines and the gesture that figures them without allowing them to be self-enclosed systems. It is this complex that allow the image to be more than a simulacrum for Merleau-Ponty and to reveal the enigma of the invisible as the invisible.

What I want to show in this chapter is that this now apparent spread of the figurative is a spatial region in common to all works of art from out of which they each originate. The figurative is in this sense the reversible region belonging to all artworks. It is also that which brings into existence the structure of desire and allows it to reveal itself as itself. One could say that it is in fact *because* they originate from out of the same circuit of desire that there is reversibility between the arts. What I will show, then, is that the arts all have some basic element that arises from out of the same figurative structure in order to convey a desire that is in the process of organizing itself. It is in the basic element of the artwork that we bear witness to the circuit of desire coming into existence. The basic elements I look at here, which betray the same figurative region in the act of forming itself, are: the inscription of the word as the basic element of the literary work of art, the plasticization as the formative moment of sculpture, and the sounding as the most primal element of poetry and music. Each of these elements, finally, are self-referential in the sense that they refer only to themselves in the act of their own formation in order to reveal the brute ground of phenomenality in the manner in which it appears prior to human cognition. I will return to this again in the Concluding Remarks.

I want to begin this chapter by examining in greater detail the suggestion with which I ended the previous chapter, that the origins of text in the literary work of art and the origins of the figures in the image are simultaneous. Merleau-Ponty, through Proust, has shown that the literary work of art belongs to the same mimetology as does image and that writing "translates" what he called the "inner book" of an "amorphous perception." The text for Proust seeks to undermine what Merleau-Ponty calls the "monument" of writing, which gives the sense-structure of language a character of being "supra-temporal."[15] The text thus operates from inside the same surfeit of determinations as does the image and forces us to see it not on the basis of the ideal structure of language that accords with a set of mental propositions: "we do not pose a goal in language," Merleau-Ponty writes, "but the goal is what we are lacking."[16] The entirety of Proust's *Recherche* is to write a novel that betrays an originary significance that fills the space of predestination in language. It could be said that the literary work, for Proust, returns to the ontological functioning of significance in order to let language reveal itself as fundamentally indeterminate and lacking of any fixed goal. The text of the literary work of art, we can thus say, inevitably functions for Proust in the way that the canvas does for Merleau-Ponty: it conveys a present meaning that reposes against the background of an original significance.

To make the claim that text and image are simultaneous, and thus that the text does not oppose itself to the image, as it is sometimes thought to do, Stephen Watson points out that Merleau-Ponty might have also emphasized Klee's "script pictures" of the 1920s. These canvases, for Klee, "take as their subject matter the equivalence between writing and drawing, between the poem and picture such that the fusion between the architectonic and the poetic become writ large."[17] One witnesses there on the canvas the threshold between hand and text. This inner-relation between hand and text, of course, carries through 20th Century art. In the pictures of Jean-Michel Basquiat, for instance, one can read words without any strenuous effort inside the image. Their meanings, however, are consistently obscured; they are endlessly crossed out, written again and corrected, emphasized and obliterated. Sometimes the texts are orphaned, appearing alongside machine parts, parts of speech, exclamatory symbols, trailing lines, graphs, etc. The text insists on marginality in the sense that it defends against the reign of any fixed determinations, and here it is brought into relation with the image. Thus, as Galen Johnson writes in a particularly striking sentence: "we need a more subtle blend of positive and negative in a language, thought and interworld that is more suggestive and flexuous, like the colours of Cézanne. We need word lines that are as philosophically compelling as the lines of Klee's drawings are aesthetically compelling."[18]

The text, like the painting, brings into the external world an interior life. It renders otherwise ideal objects in terms of the "sensible" and "public."[19] This rendering of the interior into the public shows that writing-down is fundamentally mimetic in Merleau-Ponty's sense. The text does not convey an ideal meaning but rather confers into existence the same openness of which the figurative is constitutive. The text, I thus want to say, is thereby connected to an expressive gesture that figures invisibility into visibility, and, at the deepest level, it operates by fashioning or modelling an alterior ground in order to bring it into a specific relief.

Inscribing

"[T]here is a 'hand,'" Heidegger says in his *Parmenides* lectures, "only where beings as such appear in un-concealedness and man comports himself in a disclosing way towards beings."[20] The hand, in other words, betrays a special relation to Being, a form of relatedness to Being that belongs only to the human. There is a hand in Heidegger's sense only in the relation to Being that brings it from out of its original dissimulation. The hand thus becomes implicated in Heidegger's meditations on poetic thinking and the belonging-together of *Eröterung* and *Ereignis*, between a place and the thing itself that is to be thought. The poetic for Heidegger is the appropriation of an event, in other words, where appropriation names the realm in which world and things are gathered into their *Wesen* and *Anwesen*, and it is the hand – in particular the inscribing-hand – that does this gathering. In this sense, Heidegger says, "the hand acts [*Die Hand handelt*]," for only with the inscribing-hand can their be the "Being, word, gathering, writing," that "denote an original essential nexus."[21] "In handwriting," he says again, "the relation of Being to man, namely the word, is inscribed in beings themselves."[22] And again: "the essential correlation of the hand and the word as the essential distinguishing mark of man is revealed in the fact that the hand indicates and by indicating discloses what was concealed . . ."[23]

When words are typed, then, the inscribing-hand and its relation to Being are interrupted, according to Heidegger, and this marks a "transformation in the relation of Being to man."[24] Referring to a phrase from the Greek poet Pindar, Heidegger speaks of the typed word as a "signless cloud," a covering over or "withdrawing concealment" of Being on account of the typewriter's "obtrusiveness" between handwriting, word and Being.[25] The typed word conveys a, "veiling essence," or an, "oblivion."[26] By typing the word instead of inscribing it there is a "darkening," Heidegger says again, in which "the things themselves, the aspect they present and the regard of viewing that aspect – in short, things to man – no longer stay and move in their originally arisen light."[27] In handwriting – and this is where inscriptions really bring into disclosure what was previously concealed – each word has to be written in such a way as to be pregnant with the words that have come before it and that are to follow it. Because it loses its connection to the hand that inscribes, the typed word, on the other hand, loses its connection to the possibility of disclosing, and therefore Heidegger thinks it achieves a distance from world-disclosure. The typewriter, for him, is not only a symptom of the falling away of Being but also a further entrenchment of this fallenness. No doubt Heidegger would have an even dimmer view of the computerized word that can be cut and pasted in large portions, and in doing so typed without attention paid to the poetic in language that belongs to the hand. The computer, we may say, lets us think that language is instead merely blocks of information.

I would say that the expressive gesture brings into better focus the originary nexus of word and being. The gesture is incited by an event in being. It does not resolve to imitate this origination but rather to bear it, carry it and bring it into disclosure. It is precisely this now aroused significance in the gesture that also acts on language and forces it to open up into an indeterminacy beyond signification. All words, we may say, bare the trace of a gesture that figures this indeterminacy. All words imply inscriptions. This is what Mallarmé suggests when he says that, "meditating without leaving any traces becomes evanescent," that, "[y]our act is always applied to paper," or that "man pursues black on white."[28] All inscriptions, insofar as they are reliant on an alterior ground in order to be, are also "excriptions." They show the hand in relation with an alternate surface.[29] But they will also show that this alternate surface cannot be dismissed and that it functions in the meaning of the inscription. The inscribed word thus allows us to witness a place wherein the word opens up to a sense other to it, namely the tactile.

It is Mallarmé in particular who famously became obsessed with the role of the white page in the poem. In his last great experimental poem, *Un coup de Dés jamais n'abolira le hasard*, he mocks the arbitrary rectangle of the book such that the page ceases to be linear: the words relate to each other both horizontally and vertically in order to highlight the white page. It is this white backdrop, for Mallarmé, which teems with promise and energy and becomes what the poem means.[30] It is not the ink, then, but the page that suspends the poem and expresses its state of poetic emergency. The page reveals that the meaning of the poem is held up by something other than the explicitly offered meaning. Thus the poem holds in abeyance, rather than nihilates or negates, an indeterminate meaning. The page of the poem thus does not express what Lacoue-Labarthe calls a "pure suspension of occurrence: a caesura or a syncope."[31] It is not, as Lacoue-Labarthe and Nancy would have it, the betrayal of a "negative dialectic," in which the poem expresses something totally estranged and "indestructible," and "unrelated to any operation, in any sense."[32] The poem is suspended by the same meaning with which hand comes into contact. There is thus a surface in the poem that can come-into-presence as the white page of the poem, the unsuspected reverse side of presence. There is even in the text of the poem, just as there is painting, a silent gesture at play and outlining the formation or figuration of invisibility in order to give birth to the poem.

Mallarmé's obsession with the blank page contests the norm of a page that frames the text as if it were a picture. He returns not only inscriptions (the act applied to paper) but even the text to its image and to the figurations of the invisible by devising the page in such a way that we rediscover a primal surface to poetry, allowing the poem to then exceed the logic of its frame since it can in principle be inscribed, moulded or congealed onto any place. The poem, in other words, always depends for Mallarmé on an arbitrary surface that gives it a certain frailty. For it is arbitrariness that dictates whether or not the poem reaches us. In Proust's *Recherché*, Marcel's letter of adieu to Albertine in which he references a Mallarmé sonnet (e.g., the line, "*M'introduire dans ton histoire*") goes undelivered when he neglects to tell Françoise how many stamps she should place on the envelope. Poems are not always unexpected; they do of course appear where we might suspect them, in books and collections. But they also turn up on serviettes, in bathroom stalls or on the walls of caves. The text, we can say, is to page as image is to rock; in both art forms there is a capriciousness that depends on the surface into which each is inscribed. This surface is not merely inert, self-enclosed and independent of the inscriptions. It functions by conveying an as yet unanticipated alterity in what is inscribed.

Plasticization

There is a text only insofar as there are figurations. It is here also, we have found, wherein the inscribed text opens upon a polyvalent image. The principle of *mimesis* at work in the image also gives account of a notion of *fingere* and its Greek equivalent *plassein/plattein*, "to figure," "to fashion," "to model," or "to sculpt." It is in this connection that we understand the surfaces of the poem and painting not as inert but as the site in which a previous formlessness comes to take on its form and become figured. This overflow of the logic of the composition allows us to see the work of art, in its origination, appearing on the basis of a surface that is encountered as the principle of meaning-making. Both the text and painting, consequently, open up into a sense that is other to it, into the sense of touch, and here we witness the possibility of literally touching an-other meaning. We witness, that is, the process of differentiation, a moving of the one out into the other, which the work of art performs.

The plastic artwork brings this differentiation to bear. The plastic artwork no longer abides by the modern sense of a location of a mass in space, but rather reveals an archaic space, what Merleau-Ponty calls a "topological" or "prosaic space." It does so in the following way: The mass of a sculpture takes up space. But this space is not a "finalism" or "*Ens realissimum*" so much as it is the "circumscribed relations of proximity" and "of envelopment," or what is otherwise described by Merleau-Ponty as a "wild *logos*" and the "brute principle" of an unfolding abysm into the present. The entity, that is, becomes a mass not by virtue of a discrete point-occupancy in space and time but rather it autofigures space. The entity is, in other words, a visible thing as it becomes-visible, an appearance from out of its own appearing, a formation that shows itself in the act of taking form or taking its own form. The mass of the sculpture refers to itself as a referent, and is self-reflexive in the sense that it refers to the very activity of space from out of which it has emerged as a being. Yet at the same time, the space of this mass also derives its spatiality – it is the fundamental condition for mass – from the mass. The prosaic or topological space of the plastic artwork is an originating out of which space and mass both have received their nature from the difference between them.

Apollinaire, the poet-spokesperson for cubism, speaks of the "forth dimension" to describe a non-Euclidean understanding of painting and perspective. In the plastic arts too, he says, there is a fourth dimension that, "represents the immensity of space eternalized in all directions at a given moment. It is space itself, or the dimension of infinity; it is what gives objects plasticity."[33] The fourth dimension refers to the cubist sculptor's desire to present us with a violence of movement through lines of force and multiple edges and a relativity of space that depends on the inside-outside exploration of form. The sculptor hopes to eliminate the ideal of solidity and replace it instead with a "sculptural zone" in order to show how the closure of volume at the same time requires it to open up into its surrounding space. The cubist sculptor, Katarzyna Kobro, for instance, wants to "sculpt space," and this means that the sculpture "has to be capable of both

unlimited penetration into space and absorbing space into itself."[34]
In order to break up the solid, she employs colour: "A solid each side
of which is of different colour," she writes in *Composition of Space*,
"ceases to be solid; it breaks up into a number of planes each of which
no longer serves to close off the solid, instead becoming a plane that
divides up space . . . Colour dematerializes solids . . . expands [*sic*]
into space, opens [*sic*] up a spatial field allied to the sculpture's
impact."[35] In Kobro's 1928 and 1929 models, *Spatial Composition (3)*
and *Spatial Composition (5)* the blue colour of the sky has been overcome by the sculptures' system of colour and freed from the background colour of the sky.[36] The colour into which the sculpture
enters, white, stands as the representation of a fourth dimension.
There is the sense that the sculpture penetrates and is penetrated,
opens and is opened by a dimensionality that is not merely the mea-
sured height, weight or depth of its mass. The sculpture is plastic and
voluminous since it enters into the space of infinity, which is to say,
extends outward and in all directions at once.

The infinity in volume does not reveal the "absolute distance" in
Sartre's descriptions of the Giacometti sculpture in which the sculpted
distant woman "keeps her distance even when we touch her with our
fingertips."[37] It is true that distance always eviscerates detail in a
Giacometti sculpture, and thus that there is something of the mass
that always escapes us no matter how close we get – even if we touch
it. Still, the always-postponed "expectancy" inherent in the solid will
not, as Sartre says, solve "the problem of unity within multiplicity by
simply suppressing multiplicity."[38] Rather, if we apply the concrete
logic of appearing to the plastic artwork, we discover instead that
unity does not so much suppress multiplicity as it is what coheres
multiplicity by underlying it. The sculpture conveys distance, that is,
only because its mass is an opening up into something more than
itself, a distance that is *to be* touched by our fingertips – and thus it
defines itself by the difference between space and mass. This apparition of the very difference between space and mass is inherent to the
notion of space sculpture. Sculpture is freed from the weight of a
solid when its plasticity can be seen from within a convection that
is not the erasure of the solid's particularity. In Kobro's case, cubist
sculpture is derived from the work of Futurists, and the work of

Boccioni in particular, who typically uses concavities in his models in order to free them of their own volume and link them instead with their surrounding and supporting space. This support is in turn typically conceived as a movement or inner-motion for the sake of the mass. Brancusi, another Futurist, typically uses sleek streamlined shapes and polished surfaces in order to remind us of swift movement. His models in particular carry further Rodin's idea of preceding and succeeding temporal moments conveyed by the mass.[39] A work like Auguste Rodin's *She Who Was Once the Helmet-makers Wife* is a view of the progression of old age shown by, "the masses that are kept loose and flowing, uninhibited by dry hard detail, yet suggestive of skeletal protuberances, arthritic joints, and tired sagging flesh . . . the expressive signs of age indicate the figure is subject to the vicissitudes of our environment."[40]

The dimension that gives the Rodin its plasticity, I want to say, is more like the infinity that we find in Husserl's *Space and Thing* lectures of 1907:

Space is an infinite manifold of possible locations and thereby offers a field of infinitely many possibilities of movement. Each thing is moveable *a priori* as a fulfilled spatial body and is so *in infinitum*. Therefore the possibility must be guaranteed *a priori* that movement can be given, i.e., can come to presentation . . . To this is added the possibility in principle of an ever renewed process of expansion, so to speak, of the adumbrations which the parts and the parts of the parts can undergo *in infinitum*, and through whose identifying enrolment into the schema of the whole, the respective total presentation, and finally every partial presentation as well, stand there every again as incomplete and capable of completeness.[41]

The infinite here is an infinitude of spatiality. It is the concatenation of actual and possible presentations that are ever renewable and extended *ad infinitum*, allowing the phenomenon to emerge from out of an infinite manifold of possible locations. A mass reposes against an infinitude that is the condition for its mass. Such infinitude, Husserl remarks in his notes on earthly space, is not "posited conceptually as infinite" and is instead an "existing infinite world . . . the openness as horizonality that is not completely conceived, represented but that is already implicitly formed."[42] The inner-movement of earthly space, Earth as *Ur-Arché*, articulates a sense of the infinite since each present phenomenon is a wholly contingent fact precisely because of its ever-renewing possible alternate presentations. Rodin's sculptures (his horses in particular) are able to "bestride time," Merleau-Ponty says, precisely because they betray a "mutual confrontation of incompossibles," which "cause transition and duration to arise in bronze and on the canvas."[43] A Rodin sculpture gives movement, in other words, because it actualizes the, "fictive linkages between the parts" of a solid, showing the solid presentation on the basis of one possible renewed alternate presentation that also implicitly informs the actual presentation. Infinitude in this sense is in fact a profound reduction to the appearance of a thing from its own inside out. The fourth dimension of space is not an external logic from the formation of a solid; it is instead an ultra-sensitivity for the concrete logic of incarnation, a mass that figures space and a space that figures the mass.

The figure struggles to be itself, to be own mass from within a space. This space, in turn, is not space in-itself. There is, rather, a structure of transcendence between mass and space such that the mass is not a positive presentation set against the pure negation of its space. What is positively presented in the work does not literally re-present its negative. Rather, the negative is the indirectly indicated content of the present scene. It is this basic polemic (or *polemos*, strife) between space and mass that the plastic artwork highlights and in fact gives the work its deeply pathic character. The transcendence of the two terms – space and mass – into one another confers into existence the more fundamental ontological structure of desire. That is, not just the singularity of desire but the path this desire takes into its ground as well as the indefatigable openness of this ground.

It can be pointed out that, following Lacan's reading of Merleau-Ponty and Cézanne, the sculpture bears the structure of *das Ding*, which is "the drawing of a form around a space of nothingness," or a "void," or "empty core."[44] The sculpture "must be seen as signifying structures created and shaped in relation to a void." It is pregnant with an "interior secret" that has "assumed [*sic*] the guise of a foreign body, out of place and unassimilated."[45] The sculpture, finally, is "an *extimate monument* harbouring a hollow space, a strange void which spans the poles of interiority and exteriority."[46] This structure, it must be said, confers an otherwise hidden nullity of things into the world. The mass, now revealing a frailty of its solidity, becomes both thing and non-thing at once. Francis Ponge writes that the Giacometti figure is, "at once torturer and victim . . . at once hunter and prey . . . reduced to a thread – in the dilapidation and misery of the world."[47] It is possible to conceive this *pathos* as operant in sonority.

Sounding

Merleau-Ponty has been criticized extensively for his apparently flippant relation to music at the beginning of "Eye and Mind": "Music," he infamously writes is, "too far on the hither side of the world to depict anything but certain schemata of Being – its ebb and flow, its growth, its upheavals, its turbulence."[48] This is against such renderings of seeing in those same passages: "Vision alone teaches us that beings are different, 'exterior,' foreign to one another, are yet absolutely *together*, are 'simultaneity'."[49] If not to express the thinker's ocularcentrism, these passages are taken to at least express his negligence of music, his bias and simple preference for other, non-sonorous art forms. It apparently matters not to Merleau-Ponty that sounds can differentiate things (different sounds emanate from different things) at the same time as they bring those things into cohesion (sounds cannot exist in a vacuum). But in fact references to sonority are everywhere littered in Merleau-Ponty's writings. He speaks of the "silence of being," for instance, against which there alternately stands the "noise of the world" or the "sonorous world." It may not be immediately evident, but I think the aural can be woven into the tangible and the visual in the following way.

Merleau-Ponty has already shown that a topological or prosaic space discloses the same force that bears on language, and this brings to the light of day a rupture of the system of language by a sculpturality and tangibility that is alter to it. It is not only that the inscription of a poem, for example, evokes a sense of plasticity beyond the page, the plasticity of an arbitrary surface that allows the text to function beyond the logic of the two-dimensional page. For Mallarmé, this sculpturality also demonstrates that the text of the poem is, in the poet's words, *suspended*. The sculptural operates in the meaning of the poem precisely as a suspense that is not yet determined. The poem is by definition hung, as Agamben says in *The End of the Poem*, and this same hanging happens in the schism between sound and sense, between semiotic event (e.g., rhythm as the repetition of sound) and semantic event, or between metrical series and syntactical series.[50] If suspense is its formal structure, if the poem is defined as an enjambment, prolongation or hesitation between sound and sense, then it is in a state of crisis as a matter of principle.[51] The poem's form, after all, would have to end precisely at the final strophe, when the tension between sound and sense that previously animated and intensified it no longer exists and thus when form finally shows itself as indistinguishable from content.[52] It is then, upon finishing a poem and when its form collapses into content, that we not only discover an elaboration of the linguistic tension between semiotic and the semantic but also that, beyond this, the poem projects itself towards some end – into the silence after its last verse – in which sonority and sense may finally pass into one another. And it is only at this point that the poem reveals its unique goal: it means to let the silence of language finally communicate itself without having to speak through what is said.

As a suspended being, the poem may be attuned to silence in a special way but, as we learn from reading "Indirect Language and the Voices of Silence," this silence is present in language generally as what is indirectly communicated in the said. The sense that grasps this mute background of language, we learn there, is not a separate entity out of time but contained in *praxis*, in phonemics and the mouth's ability to sound words out. The felicitous distinction that Merleau-Ponty makes in *Phenomenology of Perception* between "spoken speech" (*parole parlée*), the repetition of a language given to us, and "speaking speech" (*parole parlante*), the power of original speaking, also indicates the sign-system's dependency on sonority. Towards the end of the fourth section of *The Visible and The Invisible* this originary power of *praxis* is extended in order to show what is on the thither side of speech, about which speech speaks. There, Merleau-Ponty first refers to the noematic sense in Husserlian thought as a broadening of the notion of linguistic sense so as to include sensibility within "the special domain of language," a sensibility that grasps the "birth of meaning, or a wild meaning."[53] Thereafter he refers to the enigma of reversibility within the sonorous: "language is everything," he writes in a reference to Valéry, "since it is the voice of no one, since it is the very voice of things, the waves, and the forests."[54] He writes elsewhere in these same passages that there is a, "new reversibility and the emergence of flesh as expression are the point of insertion of speaking and thinking in the world of silence."[55]

These last remarks are evidence of a further extension of linguistic sense. Merleau-Ponty acknowledges that the sonorous within language cannot stay only at the level of speaking. If we say that words are *sounds* we admit that they are dependent on the primacy of voice, which is not only speech. The voice includes grunting, singing, crying, laughing, moaning, etc., and it implicates more directly the throat, the larynx, vocal chords, the tongue, the lips, the mouth, the lungs (inhaling, exhaling), the nose, etc. It also betrays intonation, inflection, rhythm, beat, metre, timing, etc. The voice does not itself "say something," it does not itself produce meaning; it proves instead to express something strangely recalcitrant that is not merely reducible to what is being said. The voice conveys what Merleau-Ponty previously referred to in *Signs* as the "animal of words," the sound of words that enters into the natural world. The voice is, in other words, laid open to what Merleau-Ponty has called, "open vortexes in the sonorous world" that "finally form one sole vortex . . . "[56] It is at this point laid open to a primeval silence that is the ground against which we come to hear anything at all – the wind, the air, the ocean, the birds, etc. etc. Finally, the voice will bring us even further and into the "elements," which are "not objects but fields, subdued being, nonthetic being, being before being."[57]

The excessive tension between the semiotic and the semantic in the poem gives way to the primacy of a sonority, where sonority, as suggested in these comments on the voice, will also lapse into a more profound silence of being. The reader will notice, however, that these last passages refer to the little phrases of the violin sonata. It is music, in fact, which for Merleau-Ponty conveys the thither side of the voice. He writes in his *Nature* lectures, for instance:

> the melody sings in us much more than we sing it; it goes down the throat of the singer, as Proust says. Just as the painter is struck by a painting that is not there, the body is suspended in what it sings: the melody is incarnated and finds in the body a type of servant.[58]

The notion that incarnation is servile to melody, that the body "sings," reminds us of Merleau-Ponty's comment towards the end of *The Visible and the Invisible*, in reference once again to the little phrases of the violinist, that the "performer is no longer producing and reproducing the sonata" so much as he is "at the service of the sonata" and thus "the sonata sings through him or cries out so suddenly that he must 'dash his bow' to follow it."[59] There is a melodiousness below the voice, below the singer, "below the delicate line of the violin-part," as Proust writes, which is a "liquid rippling of sound, multiform but indivisible, smooth yet restless, like the deep blue tumult of the sea, silvered and charmed into a minor key by the moonlight."

How does this basic melodiousness reveal moonlight? How does the sonorous work of art penetrate into the fundamental silence of things? John Cage refused to distinguish noises – creaking chairs, coughing, audiences shuffling, a performer's breathing, movement, etc. – from the sounds of his compositions, and this is why for him the audible also becomes an interrogation of what is *not* the composition to the extent that it includes the visible, the tangible, etc. The penetration of the alternate senses into sonority is possible not merely because a thing will convey a sound if it emanates from something that can in principle be touched or because it in some sense must occupy space. Merleau-Ponty's repeated use of the word "vibration" (as in "the vibration of things" or "ontological vibration") may well refer to the core of the thing in which there is overlap between the sonorous, the tactile and the visible. No sense has come to be from out of its own, and each passes into the other so that we may refer to this other as its reverse side. In the sonorous, in other words, there is an inarticulability and muteness that belongs as much to the tangible and the visible.

The sonorous artwork becomes an art of silence, where silence joins with intangibility, invisibility, etc. This means, too, that even the sonorous art is a work of spatiality in which a tactile and voluminous mass is figured for the listener. A recording entitled *Music and Dance* is particularly illuminating here. The recording features a guitarist (Derek Bailey) playing for a dancer (Min Tanaka) in what was apparently a glass-ceilinged, abandoned forge in Paris. On the recording, Bailey's abstract playing accompanies the sounds of Tanaka's dancing, his feet on the cement floor, his body pressing against walls, etc. A heavy rainstorm erupts, momentarily covering over the sounds of the performance, and thereafter the listener also hears the torrents of raindrops falling from a leaky roof. Bailey stops playing, from time to time, in order to let the dripping inhabit the foreground, at which point we also take notice of the sound of passing cars in a distance along with Tanaka's movements, which are near. *Music and Dance* becomes more than a recording of music, the sounds of the guitar emerge for the listener no less from the figurations of another's movements.

The recording can in fact deepen our understanding of what Merleau-Ponty calls the "awesome birth of vociferation," the mutuality and "reflexivity" of sonority in which one's "the movements of phonation" are at the same time another's "sonorous inscriptions."[60] *Music and Dance* shows that sonorous inscriptions include more than just the "motor echo" of the aural mechanisms in a hearer.[61] There is also in the recording a gestural space in which the sonorous can resonate, a figurative space that allows sonority to take place. 20th Century composition often makes reference to what is called "sound sculpture," and the phrase is not just allusory. This sonorous work of art understands itself to really take place within the format of concrete incarnation. The "*objet sonore*" is returned to a musical event that expresses more than what is contained in the words "theme," "phrase," "chord" or "chord-progression," "harmony," "melody." It aims to retrieve the sound structures contained within the robust space of a perceptual situation. (Hence the aim of *musique concrète*, the compositional organization of recorded sounds on tape). It aims to return to the concrete workings of sound.

This return to the site-specific sound understands things to be figurative such that they can be figured anew along with the vibrations of a sound. Things really do have a depth or hollow to which the present resonating sound refers in an oblique way. This referral to the hollows of the thing is a sort of re-echo of the sonorous that continues along a path, reverberating all the way into the depths of the figurative thing and back out. Here the sonorous transmits the very structure of transcending, running beneath the same and its other, in order to follow a profoundly pathic circuit that takes place between the two and binds them. In the sonorous, Merleau-Ponty says, I am always drawn "close enough to the other who speaks to hear his breath" in order that I can "feel" in the breath of the other, "his effervescence and his fatigue."[62] I find not the other as such but her palpating vitality, what Merleau-Ponty refers to in "Eye and Mind" as the "inspiration" and "expiration" of her participation in being. This exhalation joins with the figurations of plasticity in announcing the *pathos* in the uprising of things, in announcing the sudden and polemic quality of the space around those things, its structural filaments, modulations, segregations, restrictions.

Concluding Remarks

In *L'oeil et l'oreille*, Dufrenne objects to Merleau-Ponty's conception of imagination as exclusively visual. According to Dufrenne, painting for Merleau-Ponty renders the tangible only *en image*, and thus subsumed by the primacy of vision. Dufrenne's own work is dedicated to a project that he thinks remains uncritical in Merleau-Ponty's notion of reversibility, that reversibility should in fact imply some common root between the various senses, some first state of the sensible that allows for multiple associations and affinities between sensations, or what Dufrenne calls a "trans-sensibility." Reversibility must also imply a notion of the trans-artistic. A Titian or Bronzino, for example, does not simply convert the tactile into the visual, but actually evokes in us the sensibility of lush furs and soft velvets that are to be stroked, and it is this evocation by the artwork that interests Dufrenne in *L'oeil et l'oreille*. But it is indeed true for Merleau-Ponty that reversibility implies a trans-sensible realm. Reversibility, Merleau-Ponty shows in his reflections in the fourth section of *The Visible and the Invisible* on the tangible, the sonorous, the visible, etc., is a polyvalent notion. It implies the visual moving out and into the tactile, and the tactile coming forth for the sake of vision, in order that, at a more primal level, the image includes the plastic. The exclusive role of vision in imagery is thereby transgressed, is defiant of the logic of a flat surface, appearing as an image from out of the alternate sensibility of tangibility.

I have also tried to show that, according Merleau-Ponty, this region of trans-sensibility serves as the grounding for language. Though language may strive towards the elucidation of the otherwise indeterminate image in order to fix it, in fact language is fundamentally held up by indeterminacy. It is this basic indeterminacy inherent to language that the literary work of art reveals precisely because it presents itself

not as fact but as facts newly structured. This is perhaps most obvious
when the literary work of art reflects on its own structure – as both
Proust and Mallarmé's work do in different ways – in order to reveal
its own ultimate failure to parse out clarity. In this act of self-reflection,
then, the literary work of art reveals its closeness to the indeterminacy of the image. It is in this context that the logic, and text, of the
book may be understood anew. No longer taking itself to render clear
the otherwise indeterminate image, text, especially in the context of
the literary artwork, functions to reveal the polyvalent ground out of
which it has emerged. The text of the work thus does not merely
reduce itself to an image that is to be seen, but rather it brings into
presence a supporting surface that is in fact tangible and present to
touch. Finally, the literary work of art allows us to witness a region of
differentiation in which there are polysemic associations between the
various senses.

The senses, Merleau-Ponty says, betray at the deepest level an
"incessant escaping," a "shift," or a "spread."[1] They "slip away at the
very moment they are about to rejoin."[2] In the touch, for example,
there is an "impotency to superpose exactly upon one another the
touching of the things by my right hand and the touching of this
same right hand by my left hand."[3] In the sonorous, too, I witness this
process of escape and impossibility of superpositioning in "the audi-
tory experience of my own voice and that of other voices . . . because
I hear myself both from within and from without."[4] The sensible
will never catch up with itself, I find. It always runs out in front and
behind itself since it is supported by an indefatigable process of non-
coincidence or differentiation. It is with this differentiating process,
I also find, that there is in each sensible a region of confluence and
inter-penetrability. At the profoundest region in which each sense
escapes itself I thus discover, "the transition and the metamorphosis
of the one experience into the other," I discover "the hinge between
them, solid, unshakeable . . . irremediably hidden from me."[5] The
reversibility and differentiation between senses, Merleau-Ponty continues, is the more latent mode of being in which, "my flesh and that
of the world therefore involve clear zones, clearings, about which
pivot their opaque zones . . . "[6]

Phenomenology and the Obscure

Each "clear zone" or "clearing" of the sensible – the thing brought out of its previous dissimulation, made to be seen, heard, touched, etc. – cannot at the same time escape the "opaque zone" that circumambulates the particular clearing. In such descriptions of the proximity between the clear and the obscure, we are perhaps reminded of Merleau-Ponty's comments in the famous Preface to *The Phenomenology of Perception*. Phenomenology, he tells us there, is by definition paradoxical: its rigour lies in showing that the pure eidetic seeing after which it seeks cannot in the end be accomplished. In *The Visible and the Invisible*, after rediscovering these opaque zones of the phenomenon that lay beyond eidetic seeing Merleau-Ponty immediately returns again to Husserl:

> When Husserl spoke of the horizon of the things – of their exterior horizon, which everybody knows, and of their "interior horizon," that darkness stuffed with visibility of which their surface is but the limit – it is necessary to take the term seriously. No more than are the sky or the earth is the horizon a collection of things held together, or a class name, or a logical possibility of conception, or a system of "potentiality of consciousness": it is a new type of being, a being by porosity, pregnancy, or generality, and he before whom the horizon opens is caught up, included within it. His body and the distances participate in one same corporeity or visibility in general, which reigns between them and it, and even beyond the horizon, beneath his skin, unto the depths of being. [7]

Because it does not just appropriate and extend a Husserlian notion but rather makes a direct claim about Husserl's own phenomenology, this passage prompts a question about phenomenology's general relation to the obscure, the answer to which has bearing on the key role artwork plays in phenomenology. First, it may not be clear how Husserl would want to retrieve a "new type of being, a being by porosity," or the "depths of being," since his phenomenology aims to refrain from the ontological. When Husserl speaks of the "new regions of being" in *Ideas I*, for instance, this being (in the sense of "*Sein*") should be understood only as a verb. It highlights phenomenology's rediscovery of objectivity as experienceable, or the object defined solely by the way in which its phenomenality operates or functions for a subject in experience. Even the notion of the "interior horizon" or a horizon-consciousness that streams out into the "exterior horizon" or a horizon of objective appearings leads Husserl to argue for an inner or absolute time of consciousness. Granted, consciousness here has the form of time but still the operation of phenomenality, for Husserl, will always present itself not only in its facticity but also as a matter in principle, where this principle is neither arbitrary nor private but rather determined by a subjectivity as such or transcendental subjectivity.

Though it is true that over the course of his thought, eidetic phenomenology becomes in the final analysis a genetic phenomenology in which Husserl discovers the morphological historicity of the origins of thought in the life-world, it is also true that Husserl always insists on the grasping of these essential structures of subjectivity. The discovery of a transcendental subject remains a guiding principle of Husserl's thinking right through to the *Crisis of the European Sciences* and to his "Ursprung" essay of 1934 (to which Merleau-Ponty makes reference above). He is not content to remain within the metaphorical: the origins of a subject's thinking must follow an internal logic and cannot be merely chaotic; and there *really* must be an act that grasps what is essential to this subjectivity. In the language first inaugurated by *Ideas I*, the natural sciences may be concerned with real objects (or things), while a systematic philosophy may be concerned with non-real objects (or *irreal* things), which are in contradistinction to the real, such as perfectly definite forms of Being. But a rigorous science such as phenomenology is concerned with immanent essences (*Wesen*), which, although they are the pure essences or the essential nature of the *irreal* forms of Being, are what ground contingent facts. Husserl refuses to deny objectivity to these essences (though he does not say they are "real" objects), and hence for him they must also be perceivable by an act of seeing, which he calls "intuition."

How can there be obscurity in phenomenology when there is an intuition that renders the logic of experience with absolute clarity?

The emblematic title of § 75 of *Ideas I*, "Phenomenology as Descriptive Theory of the Essence of Pure Experiences,"[8] seems to be enough to problematize Merleau-Ponty's characterization of obscurity in phenomenology. It implicates phenomenology, by definition, as a descriptive study of the necessary structures of lived experience. It does not hope to explain the phenomenon by ignoring it, by postulating some hidden infrastructure or causal superstructure. It aims instead to return to the logic of the phenomenon itself and to articulate this logic in full clarity. It is in this sense, not as a perverted empirical study that imports extra-empirical sources, that phenomenology seek after the structures of experience. What the phenomenologist calls truth, according to Husserl, is just a faithful articulation of the structures of the subject, clearly grasped in intuition. There is no reality of ideal objects duplicating a world of physical objects. Only experience, not the entity apart from experience, has structure and meaning, and this means that its intelligibility lies solely within its confines. To study the phenomenon phenomenologically thus means to study it as intelligible in such a context, describing it rigorously as actually, concretely given. Even the legitimacy of a systematic speculative philosophy, according to Husserl, will depend on its adoption into the acts that ground the phenomenon. Any systematic speculative philosophy must therefore rest on the discovery of an essence within experience and the acts that grasp *eidos*. Only the science of perfectly clear apprehensions will ground "systematic inductive procedures" and "mediate inferences."[9]

Though on the face of it this sketch of early phenomenology seems contrary to Merleau-Ponty's remarks above, in fact we do not have to look to Husserl's later works to see that phenomenology is by no means a hermetically sealed field of study in which everything is grounded by absolute clarity. At the same time that even the so-called classical phenomenology of *Ideas I* is described primarily as a grasping of the essence of experience itself, Husserl also tells us a few pages earlier in § 69 that what is "given to us at the moment has a determinable margin, not yet determinable . . . a process of unfolding."[10] We also find him employing the kind of language that catches Merleau-Ponty's attention: there are in every present phenomenon, "features left confused and obscure," he writes.[11] In what may be a rare reference to Freudian psychology, he furthermore speaks of a "zone of obscure apprehension" of presentations that, "due to psychological resistances," cannot "pass over the threshold" of perfectly clear consciousness.[12] These remarks in §69c, together with the above references from §§75 f–h, force two main points. First, Husserl may be himself interested and focused on the extension of a positive philosophy into phenomenology, but this does not preclude studies of the obscure – such as that which we also find in hermeneutics – from phenomenology. Second, the consequent legitimacy of investigations of the zone of the obscure may not change the ultimate goal of phenomenology, which for Husserl remains clear vision; but neither does this mean that the obscure can be transformed into clarity. Husserl in fact redeems the obscure, qua obscurity, since he includes it within the principle of clarity, as germane to yet alienated from clear vision: "What is obscurely presented comes closer to us in its own peculiar way," he writes.[13]

"It is as though the most general character, the genus were fully given, but not as yet the difference," Husserl further writes.[14] It is thus possible here for him to distinguish a level of "pre-affectivity" that has not yet "penetrated" into explicit awareness and yet forms the background and valleys relative to the "raised saliency (*Abhebung*)" belonging to the more prominent features of explicit experience.[15] Thenceforward, we might say, there is an unknowability of differentiation – the obscure zone from out of which differentiation takes place – embedded within the field of appearing, where this unknown is not simply delimited from phenomenality. It is included (*Eingrenzung*) in phenomenology as that which is excluded (*Ausgrenzung*). It refers to me as that which may presently escape me but still has the power to exert its own overwhelming character over me in order to catch my attention.

The basic insight that the unclear cannot simply be excluded in the sense of delimited has guided subsequent studies in phenomenology (not only Merleau-Ponty but also Heidegger and Ricoeur, et al.), which have made it impossible to ignore un-presented contents within the science of presentations. For presentations, as Merleau-Ponty says, are at bottom "chiaroscuri" (*clairs-obscurs*). There is an obscurity prolonged beneath the things of the world and further still beneath the particular sky and earth, where particulars are not yet clearly particulars. The first sudden appearance of a being comes forth from this intervalent depth as if emerging from the subtle line between sky and earth, a subtlety that is itself subsumed neither by that sky nor by that earth – a region in which their difference is not yet known. Husserl's radical claim, according to Merleau-Ponty above, is that consciousness is in a fundamental way included, even caught up, in this intervalent depth so that relations of distance – far, near, here, there – are not yet known to it.

Art and the Obscure

Merleau-Ponty's rediscovery of the opaque zone within the clear zone, or of obscurity within the clearing, forces him to problematize, following Husserl, the notion of a transcendental structure that would render the obscure lucid. He furthermore retrieves this obscurity, which is included in one's ownmost being, by interrogating the origins of the work of art. The work emerges from out of itself in order to present an obscure zone that would have otherwise remained irremediably hidden from me, a region in which difference (for instance, the different senses) is not yet known. This does not mean that the work now renders an otherwise obscure contradiction in such a way as to be reconciled in positive terms. It rather approaches me in its own symbolic terms so that it may articulate its own being as the opaque. The artwork thus autofigures its own structures for me and usurps the place of an eidetic doctrine of pure mental processes. It accomplishes itself, furthermore, precisely as that which is unclear. This is, to borrow Husserl's phrase above, the obscure coming closer to us in its own peculiar way. This propinquity of the obscure goes well beyond what Max Ernst calls "decorative amusement" or "the pure invention of felt reality." For, if the artwork invents, its inventions are at the same time discoveries, revelations. The work discloses the logic of phenomenality itself, bares itself from its own inside out. It offers itself from out of the auspices of its own disclosure. Here the work is that with which I am not immediately identical, not immediately simultaneous. It is prior to me, and prior to my ability to consume it. But, since this foreignness is also my ownmost being, the artwork's priority to me is only to the extent that it first catches me up in its depth in order for it to appear. This point needs reiteration: *the aesthetic, for Merleau-Ponty, is the obscure presenting itself as obscure, thereby calling me into question by catching me up into its obscurity.*

How can the work achieve itself before me? Imagine what a viewer might undergo in front of the artwork. The work initially gives its most rudimentary elements. If it is a painting, at first the work is not more than a series of small, singular expressions. Elkins says that the painting can "preserve the memory of the tired bodies that made them, the quick jabs, the exhausted truces, the careful nourishing gestures. Painters can sense those motions in the paint even before they notice what the paintings are about."[16] According to Cy Twombly, for instance, all of this is contained in the mark – a sequence of scribbles, smudges, dots, lines, etc. – whose impulse still remains exploratory, searching for a pictorial solution whose outcome is as yet unknown.[17] The rudimentary mark, the inceptive element of the artwork, this is what so-called "extended technique" of modern composition also attempts to rediscover. The still rudimentary element may give the impression of randomness, but in fact it is reflective in the extreme: a concentration of sensations, scrupulously noted but not yet fixed and still obedient to the pregnancy of the emotion and the pathic. One is no doubt tempted to search for explicit meaning; the scribbles of a Twombly may come to have apparently real figures, even words; the composition may indicate rhythm, metre, melody, etc. The viewer has now entered the world of the visible and sense. But this world is still too tentative, still too dedicated to the initial exploratory elements, to really be comprehensible. The rhythm is not more than pulsation, and the rudimentary mark of the image is "suspended between coming and going," "forever hypothetical" and "doomed to partake in an open-ended discourse on painting where marks will continue to accrue without ever arriving at a definition of painting."[18] The viewer cannot forget, cannot leave behind, the period in which the things now becoming visible were previously denuded, not yet things at all – the period in which they were instituted.

Notes

Introduction

[1] Merleau-Ponty, Maurice (1964) *Signs* (Henceforth referred to as *S*), translated by Richard C. McCleary. Evanston: Northwestern University Press, pp. 39–84.

[2] Merleau-Ponty, Maurice (1968) *The Visible and the Invisible* (Henceforth referred to as *VI*), translated by Alphonso Lingis. Evanston: Northwestern University Press.

[3] Already in the first few passages of the Preface to *Sense and Nonsense*, Merleau-Ponty writes the following: "When we confront a genuine novel, poem, painting, or film, we know that a contact has been established with something, that something has been gained for men; and the work of art begins to transmit an uninterrupted message. But the meaning of the work for the artist or for the public cannot be stated except by the work itself: neither the thought which created it nor the thought which receives it is completely its own master." Merleau-Ponty, Maurice (1964) *Sense and Nonsense* (Henceforth referred to as *SNS*), translated by Hubert L. Dreyfus and Patricia Allen Dreyfus. Evanston: Northwestern University Press, p. 3.

[4] ibid., pp. 1–25.

[5] ibid., p. 18.

[6] Paz, Octavio (1990) *The Collected Poems of Octavio Paz, 1957–1987*. New York: New Direction Books, p. 509.

[7] *SNS*, p. 14.

[8] ibid., p. 15.

[9] *S*, p. 178.

[10] *SNS*, p. 13.

[11] ibid., p. 16.

[12] Merleau-Ponty, Maurice (1964) *Primacy of Perception and Other Essays* (Henceforth referred to as *PrP*), edited by James E. Edie. Evanston: Northwestern University Press, p. 161.

[13] Elkins, James (2000) *What Painting Is*. London: Routledge Press, pp. 147–167.

[14] Jay, Martin (1993), *Downcast Eyes: The Denigration of Vision in 20th-Century French Thought*. Berkeley and Los Angeles: University of California Press, p. 24.

[15] ibid., p. 25.

[16] ibid.

[17] *VI*, p. 223.

[18] *S.*, pp. 54 & 54–5.

[19] ibid., p. 55.

[20] ibid., p. 56.

[21] Merleau-Ponty writes of *The Bathers:* "Nevertheless, Renoir was looking at the sea. And why did the blue of the sea pertain to the world of his painting? How was it able to teach him something about the brook in *The Bathers?* Because each fragment of the world – and in particular the sea, sometimes riddled with eddies and ripples and plumed with spray, sometimes massive and immobile in itself – contains all sorts of shapes of being, and, by the way it has of joining the encounter with one's glance, evokes a series of possible variants and teaches, over and beyond itself, a general way of expressing being." ibid.

[22] *VI*, p. 209.

[23] ibid., p. 210.

[24] ibid., p. 211.

[25] ibid.

[26] ibid.

[27] ibid., p. 210.

[28] Barbaras, Renaud (2009) "Métaphore et Ontologie" in *Le tournant de l'experience.* Paris: VRIN. p. 287.

[29] ibid.

[30] Dufrenne, Mikel (1987) *L'oeil et l'oreille.* Montreal: Éditions de l'Hexagone.

[31] *PrP*, p. 167 and *VI*, p. 208   The references are slightly altered in each text. I quote from *VI* in the above.

[32] *VI*, p. 209.

[33] ibid.

[34] ibid.

[35] ibid.

[36] ibid.

[37] ibid.

[38] ibid., pp. 208–9.

[39] ibid.

[40] ibid.

[41] Merleau-Ponty, Maurice (2003) *L'institution et la passivité: Notes de cours au Collège de France* (Henceforth referred to as *IP*) Paris: Editions Belin, p. 36.

[42] See Claude Lefort's Preface to ibid., p. 6.

[43] *PrP*, p. 184.

[44] Flam, Jack (1995) *Matisse on Art.* Los Angeles: University of California Press, p. 146.

[45] *VI*, p. 209.

[46] *S*, p. 20.

[47] *IP*, p. 86–7.

[48] *PrP*, p. 180.

[49] *S*, p. 166.

[50] For an insightful reflection on Merleau-Ponty's notion of bodily spatiality, in relation to the history of thought (specifically Kant and Derrida), see Russon, John, "The Spatiality of Self-Consciousness: Originary Passivity in Kant, Merleau-Ponty and Derrida" in *Chiasmi International Vol. 9.* Memphis: University of Memphis Press, pp. 219–30.

[51] *IP*, p. 88.

52 *VI*, p. 243.

53 ibid., p. 211.

54 ibid., pp. 207–8.

55 Watson, Stephen H. (2009), *In the Shadow of Phenomenology: Writings After Merleau-Ponty I*. London: Continuum Books. p. 89.

56 ibid.

57 Merleau-Ponty, Maurice (2008) "La Nature ou le monde du silence" in *Maurice Merleau-Ponty*. Paris: Hermann Éditeurs, p. 53.

58 *VI*, p. 139.

59 *IP*, pp. 63–78 and *VI*, pp. 155–9.

60 *PrP*, p. 170.

61 ibid., p. 185.

Chapter 1

1 Dillon, M. C. (1997), *Merleau-Ponty's Ontology*, 2nd *Edition*. Evanston: Northwestern University Press.

2 Merleau-Ponty, Maurice (1973), *Prose of the World* (Henceforth referred to as *PW*), translated by John O'Neill. Evanston: Northwestern University Press, 1973, p. 69.1

3 ibid., p. 106–7.

4 Dillon, *Merleau-Ponty's Ontology*, p. 205.

5 ibid.

6 ibid.

7 *S*, pp. 45–6.

8 *PW*, pp. 9–46.

9 Malraux, André (1990), *The Voices of Silence*, translated by Stuart Gilbert. New Jersey: Princeton University Press, p. 21.

10 *S*, p. 39.

11 ibid., p. 42.

12 ibid., p. 44.

13 ibid., p. 42–3.

14 ibid., p. 44.

15 ibid., p. 43.

16 *VI*, p. 144.

17 Waldenfels, Bernard (2000) "The Paradox of Expression" in *Chiasms: Merleau-Ponty's Notion of Flesh*, edited by Fred Evans and Leonard Lawlor. Albany: State University of New York Press, p. 95–6.

18 *S*. p. 64.

19 *VI*, p. 167.

20 ibid.

21 ibid., p. 201.

22 ". . . with the first phonemic oppositions the child is initiated to the lateral liaison of sign to sign as the foundation of an ultimate relation of sign to meaning – in the special form it has received in the language in question.

Phonologists have succeeded in extending their analysis beyond words to forms, to syntax, and even to stylistic differences because the language in its entirety as a style of expression and a unique manner of handling words is anticipated by the child in the first phonemic oppositions. The whole of the spoken language surrounding the child snaps him up like a whirlwind, tempts him by its internal articulations, and brings him *almost* up to the moment when all this noise begins to mean something." *S*, p. 40.

23　*VI*, p. 170.

24　ibid.

25　*S*, p. 18.

26　*PW*, p. 46.

27　*S*, p. 42.

28　ibid., p. 45.

29　Foucault, Michel (1970) *The Order of Things: An Archeology of the Human Sciences.* New York: Pantheon, p. 9.

30　ibid.

31　ibid., pp. 28–9.

32　*PW*, 46.

33　ibid.

34　Nancy, Jean-Luc (2008) *Corpus*, translated by Richard A. Rand. New York: Fordham University Press, p. 23.

35　*PW*, p. 43.

36　ibid., p. 46.

37　Malraux, *The Voices of Silence*, p. 21.

38　*S*, p. 63.

39　ibid.

40　ibid., p. 67.

41　ibid., p. 63.

42　ibid., p. 82.

43　ibid., p. 80.

44　ibid.

45　ibid., p. 65.

46　*VI*, p. 86.

47　ibid., p. 87.

48　Hegel, G. W. F (1975) *Hegel's Aesthetics: Lectures on Fine Arts Vol. II*, translated by T. M. Knox. Oxford: Oxford University Press. p. 614.

49　ibid., p. 618.

50　*S*, pp. 79–80.

51　Taminiaux, Jacques (1981) "From Dialectics to Hyperdialectics" in *Merleau-Ponty: Perception, Structure, Language*, edited by John Sallis. Atlantic Highlands: Humanities Press, p. 75.

52　*VI*, p. 191.

53　*S*, p. 62.

54　ibid., p. 69.

55　ibid., p. 20.

56　*S*, p. 59.

[57] *VI*, p. 173.

[58] ibid., p. 192.

[59] ibid., p. 243.

[60] ibid., p. 259.

[61] ibid.

[62] Steinbock, Anthony J. (2000) "Reflections on Earth and World: Merleau-Ponty's Project of Transcendental History and Transcendental Geology" in *Merleau-Ponty: Difference, Materiality, Painting*, edited by Veronique M. Foti. Amherst: Humanity Books, p. 104. Steinbock, like Merleau-Ponty before him, is making reference to Husserl's "Ursprung" text, published as Husserl, Edmund (1940) "Grundlegende Untersuchungen zum phänomologischen Ursprung der Räumlichkeit der Natur" (Henceforth referred to as "Ursprung") in *Philosophical Essays in Memory of Edmund Husserl.* Cambridge: Harvard University Press, p. 324.

[63] Steinbock, "Reflections on Earth and World," p. 105; he is referring to the "Ursprung" essay, p. 319.

[64] Vallier, Robert (2006), "Institution: The Significance of Merleau-Ponty's 1954 Lectures at the Collège de France" in *Chiasmi International Vol. 7.* Memphis: University of Memphis Press, p. 281.

[65] ibid. 298.

[66] Lyotard, Jean-François (2002), *Discours, Figure.* Paris: Klincksieck Press, p. 20.

[67] *VI*, p. 144.

[68] ibid.

[69] "Since the total visible is always behind, or after, or between the aspects we see of it, there is access to it only through an experience which, like it, is wholly outside of itself. It is thus, and not as the bearer of a knowing subject, that our body commands the visible for us, but it does not explain it, does not clarify it, it only concentrates the mystery of its scattered visibility; and it is indeed a paradox of Being, not a paradox of man, that we are dealing with here." ibid., p. 136.

[70] ibid., p. 179.

[71] ibid., p. 4.

[72] *S*, p. 59.

[73] ibid.

[74] ibid., p. 67.

[75] ibid.

[76] Jean-Luc Nancy (1996) *The Muses*, translated by Peggy Kamuf. Stanford: Stanford University Press, p. 74.

[77] *PrP*, p. 144.

[78] ibid., p. 164.

[79] ibid., p. 165.

[80] ibid.

[81] *PW*, p. 72.

[82] Nancy, *The Muses*, p. 20.

[83] ibid., p. 75.

[84] ibid.

85 ibid.

86 ibid.

87 ibid., p. 76.

88 Gaschet, Rudolf (1997) "Alongside the Horizon" in *On Jean-Luc Nancy: The Sense of Philosophy*, edited by Darren Sheppard, Simon Sparks and Colin Thomas. London: Routledge. p. 148–9.

89 ibid., p. 150.

90 Nancy, Jean-Luc (1993) *The Birth to Presence*. Stanford: Stanford University Press, p. 353.

91 ibid., p. 352.

92 Nancy, *The Muses*, p. 75.

93 *PrP*, p. 164. Greenberg explains: "The Paleolithic painter or engraver could disregard the norm of the frame and treat the surface in a literally sculptural way only because he made images rather than pictures, and worked on a support – a rock wall, a bone, a horn, or a stone – whose limits and surface were arbitrarily given by nature." Clement Greenberg (1993), *The Collected Essays and Criticism*, V.4, edited by John O'Brian. Chicago: University of Chicago Press, p. 92.

94 Crowther, Paul (2009) *Phenomenology of the Visual Arts (even the frame)*. Stanford: Stanford University Press, p. 53.

95 Wölfflin, Heinrich (1950) *The Principles of Art History: The Problem of the Development of Style in Later Art*. Mineola, New York: Dover Publications, pp. 18–19.

96 To overcome the picture-frame implies for Wölfflin a move from: the "linear line" to the "painterly line" (to dissolute the firm, plastic form with strongly stressed outlines into a quivering and flickering, moving form); from plane to recession (the development from the vision of the surface to the vision of depth); from closed to open form (the development of pictures no longer adjusted to the line of the frame but rather suggesting the representational area beyond the borders of the work); from multiplicity to unity (the development from the classic composition, in which single parts have a certain independence, to a feeling of unity); and from relative clearness to unclearness (the development from a distinctness, in which light defines form in the detail, to an attempt to evade clearness, to make the totality of the picture seem unintentional). The move from the linear to the painterly is conveyed for Wölfflin by the shift to Rembrandt and a Renaissance art from Dürer and Baroque art: "What radically distinguishes Rembrandt from Dürer is the vibration of the picture as a whole, which persists even where the eye was not intended to perceive the individual form-signs. Certainly it powerfully supports the illusive effect if an independent activity in the building up of the picture is assigned to the spectator, if the separate brush-strokes coalesce only in the act of contemplation. But the picture which comes to birth is fundamentally disparate from the picture of the linear style. The presentment *remains* indeterminate, and is not meant to settle into those lines and planes which have a meaning for the tactile sense." ibid., p. 18.

97 Nancy, *The Muses*, p. 37.

98 Elkins, *What Painting Is*, p. 72.

99 ibid.

Chapter 2

[1] The original, significantly shorter version of this chapter appears in *Analecta Husserliana CIV* 2009, pp. 77–91 under the title "*Physis* and Flesh."

[2] *PrP*, p. 167.

[3] Edmund Husserl (2003) "Foundational Investigations of the Phenomenological Origin of the Spatiality of Nature: The Originary Ark, the Earth, Does Not Move," in Maurice Merleau-Ponty, *Husserl at the Limits of Phenomenology* (Henceforth referred to as *HLP*), edited by Leonard Lawlor and Bettina Bergo. Evanston: Northwestern University, p. 127.

[4] Lingis, Alphonso (1969) "The Elemental Background" in *New Essays in Phenomenology*, edited by James M. Edie. Chicago: Quadrangle Books, pp. 24–38.

[5] Merleau-Ponty, "La Nature ou le monde du silence", p. 53.

[6] ibid.

[7] ibid., p. 147.

[8] ibid., p. 275.

[9] ibid, p. 136.

[10] *VI*, p. 267.

[11] I thus take Merleau-Ponty to have adequately responded to an important criticism made by Haar, who writes: "[t]here is not in Merleau-Ponty any radical questioning of subjectivity, in the sense of there being no 'deconstruction' of the subject which brings to light its metaphysical presuppositions and which is in dialogue with the tradition throughout which it is constituted: that is, from the mutations of the *hypokeimenon* into *substantia* and of the latter into *subjectum*." My translation. Haar, Michel (1999) *La philosophie français entre phénoménologie et métaphysique*. Paris: Presses Universitaires de France, p. 21.

[12] Heidegger, Martin (1975) *Gesamtausgabe* (Henceforth referred to as *GA*) vol. 9, entitled *Wegmarken*, edited by Friedrich-wilhelm von Herrmann. Franfkfurt am Main: Vittorio Klostermann, p. 309.

[13] The difference between the two epilogues is quoted and reflected upon in: Richardson, William J. (1973) *Heidegger: Through Phenomenology to Thought*. Reinbek: Rowohlt, p. 501; cf. pp. 500–1. I am borrowing from Richardson's argument here.

[14] *GA*, p. 309.

[15] ibid.

[16] Heidegger, Martin (1953) *Einführung in die Metaphysik* (Henceforth referred to as *EM*). Tübingen: Niemeyer, p. 115.

[17] ibid., p. 54.

[18] Heidegger, Martin (1962) *Being and Time*, translated by John Macquarrie and Edward Robinson. New York: Harper & Row Publishers, p. 51.

[19] *GA*, p. 264.

[20] ibid.

[21] Aristotle, *Metaphysics, Books I–IX*, translated by Hugh Tredennick. Cambridge: Harvard University Press (1996), 1028b.

[22] *GA* 9:274.

[23] *EM*, p. 77–8.

[24] ibid., p. 95.

[25] Aristotle, *The Physics*, Books I–IV, translated by F. M. Cornford and P. H. Wickseed. Cambridge: Harvard University Press (1996), 193 b8–12.

26 Heidegger, Martin (1964) "Lettre à Monsieur Beaufort" in *Lettre surs l'humanisme*, translated by R. Munier. Paris: Aubier, p. 182.

27 Heidegger, Martin, *Die Grundprobleme der Phänomenologie*, in *GA* volume 24, p. 444.

28 ibid.

29 *EM*, p. 47.

30 ibid., p. 48.

31 *VI*, p. 65.

32 Merleau-Ponty, Maurice (2003) *Nature: Course Notes from the Collège de France* (Henceforth referred to as *N*), translated by Robert Vallier. Evanston: Northwestern University Press, p. 204.

33 ibid.

34 ibid.

35 *VI*, 253.

36 ibid., p. 265.

37 Waldenfels, Bernard (1996) *Order in the Twilight*, translated by David J. Parent. Athens: Ohio University Press, p. 116–17.

38 Dufrenne, Mikel (1981) "Eye and Mind" in *Merleau-Ponty: Perception, Structure, Language*, edited by John Sallis. Atlantic Highlands: Humanities Press, p. 256.

39 *N*, p. 174.

40 *VI*, p. 147.

41 ibid.

42 One should also note here that the Latin word for "origin," *oriri*, also traces back to the Greek *oros*, which refers to a mountain that juts out from the surrounding country. *Oriri* itself can mean "to rise," especially in the sense of a sun or moonrise, or else it means "to have a beginning," "to spring up" or "to be born." It is thus also connected to *aboriri*, which means "to die" or "to disappear." Here the "ab-" connotes "away from" (life).

43 *VI*, p. 147.

44 ibid., p. 139.

45 *VI*, p. 181.

46 *PrP*, p. 182.

47 ibid., p. 154.

48 ibid.

49 ibid.

50 ibid., p. 155.

51 ibid.

52 One could also relate Merleau-Ponty's notion of growth, then, to Heidegger's famous descriptions of the Greek temple in "Origins of the Work of Art" in which the temple is in sharp contrast with everything else that comes to appear. Standing there, the temple opens up a world at the same time that it sets this world back again into the earth, which in this way emerges as what it is, namely, native ground. The temple thus highlights the primacy of a *topos* such that it arrives in its place and has a place before it has space. Heidegger, Martin (1975) "Origins of the Work of Art" in *Poetry, Language, Thought*, translated by Albert Hofstadter. New York: Harper & Row, p. 55.

53 *IP*, pp. 88 and 3.

54 *PrP*. p. 180.

55 *VI*, pp. 210–11.

56 *IP*, p. 80.

57 I am using Foucault's descriptions of various forms of *topos* here. Utopias, he says, "afford consolation: although they have no real locality there is nevertheless a fantastic, untroubled region in which they are able to unfold." They "open up cities with vast avenues, superbly planted gardens, countries where life is easy even though the road to them is chimerical." Foucault, *The Order of Things*, p. 48.

58 "[H]eterotopias desiccate speech, stop words in their tracks, contest the very possibility of language at its source; they dissolve our myths and sterilize the lyricism of our sentences." ibid.

59 See Visker, Rudi (1999) *Truth and Singularity: Taking Foucault into Phenomenology*. Dordrecht: Kluwer Academic Publishers. p. 103–4. See also Waldenfels' *Order in the Twilight*: "The extra-ordinary as an existing other order draws its glittering brilliance from an extraordinary that suggests *an order possible elsewhere*. This elsewhere is not to be understood as pure nowhere, as utopia, but as an atopia . . ." pp. 116–117.

60 Nancy, *The Muses*, p. 33.

61 Merleau-Ponty, Maurice (1988) "Philosophy and Non-Philosophy since Hegel" in *Philosophy and Non-Philosophy Since Merleau-Ponty*, edited by Hugh J. Silverman. London: Routledge. p. 40.

62 ibid.

63 *IP*, p. 83.

64 Merleau-Ponty, "Philosophy and Non-Philosophy Since Hegel," p. 40.

65 ibid.

66 *S*, p. 164.

67 *IP*, p. 84.

68 *PrP*, p. 183.

69 *VI*, p. 247.

70 *PrP*, p. 183.

71 ibid., p. 181.

72 ibid., p. 184.

73 ibid.

74 ibid.

75 *S*, p. 58.

76 ibid.

77 *IP*, p. 83.

78 Johnson, Galen, "Thinking in Color: Merleau-Ponty and Paul Klee" in *Merleau-Ponty: Difference, Materiality, and Painting*, edited by Veronique M. Foti. Amherst: Humanity Books, p. 170.

79 *VI*, p. 305.

80 Klee, Paul (1993) *On Modern Art* in *Art in Theory, 1900–2000: An Anthology of Changing Ideas*, edited by Charles Harrison and James Wood. London: Blackwell Publishing, p. 368.

81 *PrP*, p. 174.

82 ibid., p. 181.

83 ibid., p. 174.

84 ibid. p. 180.

85 ibid., p. 181.

86 ibid.

87 I am referring, especially, to the following passage in "Cézanne's Doubt": "If one outlines the shape of an apple with a continuous line, one makes an object of the shape, whereas the contour is rather the ideal limit toward which the sides of the apple recede in depth. Not to indicate any shape would be to deprive the objects of their identity. To trace just a single outline sacrifices depth – that is, the dimension in which the thing is presented not as spread out before us but as an inexhaustible reality full of reserves. That is why Cézanne follows the selling of the object in modulated colors and indicates *several* outlines in blue. Rebounding among these, one's glance captures a shape that emerges from among them all, just as it does in perception," *SNS*, p. 14.

88 *PrP*, p. 181.

89 Martin, David, "On Perceiving Paintings and Sculpture" in *Leonardo* Vol. 11, 1978, p. 289.

90 Klee, *On Modern Art*, p. 368.

91 ibid.

92 ibid.

93 *PrP*, p. 182.

94 Barbaras, Renaud (2005) *Desire and Distance: Introduction to Phenomenology of Perception*, translated by Paul Milan. Stanford: Stanford University Press.

95 Johnson, Galen (2010) *The Retrieval of the Beautiful: Thinking Through Merleau-Ponty's Aesthetics*. Evanston: Northwestern University Press.

96 ibid., p. 152.

97 ibid.

98 ibid.

99 *PrP*, p. 167.

100 *VI*, p. 144.

101 Merleau-Ponty writes in this connection that, "fire pretends to be alive; it awakens. Working its way along the hand as its conductor, it reaches the support and engulfs it; then a leaping spark closes the circle it was to trace, coming back to the eye, and beyond." ibid. p. 188.

102 ibid., p. 167.

103 *PrP*, p. 169.

104 *PrP*, p. 167.

105 "True," Merleau-Ponty writes of Freud's essay, "the reader is stopped more than once by the lack of evidence. Why this and not something else? The question seems all the more pressing since Freud often offers several interpretations, each symptom being 'over-determined' according to him." But, he continues, "we should not take Leonardo's fantasy of the vulture, or the infantile past which it masks, for a force which determined his future. Rather it is like the words of the oracle, an ambiguous symbol which applies in advance to several possible chains of events." *SNS*, p. 24.

[106] Dufrenne even points out that, in this analysis of the artwork, Merleau-Ponty can go so far as to say that ultimately the artwork reveals that our waking lives are filled with dream landscapes, full of unexpected significance, and thus that we are implicitly held suspended in a day that is more like dreaming a dream than waking up from one. Held in suspense of a significant object, Dufrenne writes, we move between a "daytime," when we are apparently separated from the real, and a "nighttime," when we are caught up in the swarm of an abyss or a depth. Dufrenne, Mikel (1990) *In the Presence of the Sensuous: Essays in Aesthetics.* Amherst, New York: Prometheus Books. p. 140. Here it could be said that Merleau-Ponty extends what Freud calls the "dream-day," the notion that we know nothing about the various things with which we come into contact throughout the day until we revisit them later in a dream.

[107] It is said in this connection that Picasso could never have conceived his revolutionary *Demoiselles d'Avignon* were it not for his specific act of inciting conflict. He toys with what he considers philistine notions of decency by allying himself with what the bourgeois considered taboo – prostitutes and African masks – in order that his art may in fact purge these taboos. He intentionally uses these despised objects, employing them symbolically in terms of subject matter and form, in order to allow them to transgress their conventional use-value. The painter famously finds in the Grebo mask a real potential for metaphoric extension, a series of possible images in one signifier: a single mark to show the mouth may also be an eye, or else it may be a navel. He had already insisted on the possibility of a plastic metaphoricity at the heart of cubism when first he used the decorator-painter's "comb" (normally used to imitate the grain of wood) to portray the hair of the 1912 *Le Poète.* But this plasticity can be achieved only after Picasso finally dissociates the contrast of shadow and light from its traditional function as modelling in translating sculptural qualities into painting. And it can only be achieved once Picasso understands this function as simply one pictorial code among other possible codes in order that he may freely efface the realistic image with the use of multiple, contradictory light sources and views. The effacement of the realistic image allows Picasso to paint what he feels, what he tells himself he sees.

[108] Bahr, Hermann. *Expressionism in Art in Theory 1900–2000: An Anthology of Changing Ideas,* p. 117.

[109] In particular Lyotard has in mind here artworks that are self-referential, artworks that refer to their own inner-workings that have made them possible but where these workings are not themselves to be represented. Rothko's canvases, for example, are beyond representation for Lyotard. They are the "art of art," which "ask how to determine the thought and the willed means for making the mute experience of 'I without a self' audible without violating its silence . . . The least one can say is that the ego inflicts on itself the discipline of listening before-beyond the audible, of sensitizing itself to that which is insensitive to it." Lyotard, Jean-François (2001) *Soundproof Room: Malraux's Anti-Aesthetics,* translated by Robert Harvey. Stanford: Stanford University Press. p. 46.

[110] Lyotard, *Discours, Figure,* p. 23.

[111] ibid., p. 20.

[112] *PrP*, p. 188.

[113] Merleau-Ponty writes in this context that for the painter there is a, "problem of velvet or wool," which "upsets the givens of all the other problems." ". . . [The painter's] quest is total even where it looks partial. Just when he has reached proficiency in some area, he finds that he has reopened another one where everything he said before must be said again in a different way." *VI*, p. 189.

[114] *PrP*, p. 166.

[115] ibid., 164.

[116] ibid., p. 164.

[117] *VI*, pp. 5–6.

[118] ibid., p. 26.

[119] ibid., p. 6.

[120] ibid., p. 191–2.

[121] Merleau-Ponty, Maurice (1970) *Themes from Lectures at the Collège de France 1952–1960*, translated by John O'Neill. Evanston: Northwestern Press, p. 48.

[122] ibid.

[123] *IP*, pp. 59 and 54.

[124] ibid. p. 59.

Chapter 3

[1] An earlier version of this chapter appears in *Studia Phaenomenologica Vol. VIII* (2008) pp. 121–139 under the title "Architectonic and Myth Time: Merleau-Ponty's Proust in *The Visible and the Invisible*."

[2] Casey, Edward S. (2000) *Remembering: A Phenomenological Study*. Bloomington: Indiana State University. p. 105.

[3] *VI*, p. 243.

[4] ". . . the word *Stiftung* – 'foundation' or 'establishment' – emphasizes 'the unlimited fecundity of each present" and especially describes "that fecundity of the products of culture which continue to have value after their appearance and which open a field of investigation in which they perpetually come to life again." Here Merleau-Ponty also remarks that there is "*the power to forget origins*," *S*, p. 59.

[5] ibid.

[6] *VI*, p. 173.

[7] ibid., p. 267.

[8] ibid., p. 173.

[9] Benjamin, Walter (1968), "The Image of Proust" in *Illuminations: Essays and Reflections*. New York: Pantheon Books, p. 202.

[10] Proust, Marcel (1998), *Remembrance of Things Past: Book 1 Swann's Way*, translated by Terence Kilmartin and C. K. Scott Moncrieff. New York: Penguin Classics, pp. 47–8.

[11] Morrison, James and Stack, George J., "Proust and Phenomenology" in *Man and World: An International Philosophical Review*, vol. 1, 1968, p. 605.

[12] ibid., p. 606.

[13] ibid.

[14] Hart, James G., "Toward a Phenomenology of Nostalgia" in *Man and World: An International Philosophical Review*, vol. 6 1973, p. 401.

[15] ibid.

[16] Breeur, Roland (2000) *Singularité et sujet. Une lecture phénoménologique de Proust.* Paris: Jérôme Millon, pp. 154 and 157.

[17] Merleau-Ponty, Maurice (2003) *Phenomenology of Perception* (Henceforth referred to as *PP*), translated by Colin Smith. London: Routledge Press, p. 418.

[18] *VI*, p. 168.

[19] ibid., p. 150.

[20] ibid.

[21] ibid., p. 149.

[22] ibid., p. 103.

[23] Proust, *Remembrance of Things Past*, p. 294.

[24] ibid., p. 295.

[25] *VI*, p. 159.

[26] Breeur, *Singularité et sujet. Une lecture phénoménologique de Proust*, p. 155.

[27] ibid., p. 149.

[28] Proust, *Remembrance of Things Past*, p. 277.

[29] ibid., p. 307.

[30] ibid., p. 314.

[31] ibid., p. 543.

[32] *VI* p. 261.

[33] This is a term used by Walter Biemel in his very helpful essay "Zu Marcel Proust, Die Zeit als Hauptperson," in *Philosophische Analysen zur Kunst der Gegenwart*, Phaenomenologica 28, 1968.

[34] Kristeva, Julia (1993) *Proust and the Sense of Time*, translated by Stephen Bann. London: Faber and Faber Limited. p. 7.

[35] ibid.

[36] ibid.

[37] ibid., p. 197.

[38] "Hence, if anyone loves a paradox, he can really say, and say with strict truth if he will allow for the ambiguity, that the element which makes up the life of phenomenology as of all eidetical science is 'fiction,' that fiction is the source whence the knowledge of 'eternal truths' draws its sustenance." Husserl, Edmund (1983) *Ideas Pertaining to a Pure Phenomenology and to a Phenomenological Philosophy: First Book: General Introduction to a Pure Phenomenology*, translated by Fred Kersten. Dordrecht: Springer, p. 184.

[39] *SNS*, p. 28.

[40] Kristeva, *Proust and the Sense of Time*, p. 60.

[41] See, for example, Genette, Gérard, "Métonymie chez Proust," *Figures* vol. 3, 1972.

[42] *VI*, p. 151. As M. Carbone points out, this vortex refers to "the *fungierende* or latent intentionality which is the intentionality within being." See his essay, "The Time of Half-Sleep: Merleau-Ponty between Husserl and Proust," in Carbone, Mauro (2004) *The Thinking of the Sensible: Merleau-Ponty's A-Philosophy*. Evanston: Northwestern University Press, p. 9. See also *VI*, p. 244.

[43] We might say that a thing also functions for Proust as a signifying event in Heidegger's sense, indicating the ontological structure of referential totalities and of a worldhood. See Deleuze, Gilles (2004) *Proust and Signs*. Minneapolis: University of Minnesota Press. p. 114.

[44] We can thus follow Deleuze's claim in *Proust and Signs* that the thing for Proust operates as a sign for a world in the Greek sense: "The Greek world is expressed not only in the Logos as totality, but in fragments and shreds as objects of aphorisms, in symbols as fractions, in the signs of the oracles, and in the madness or delirium of the soothsayers." ibid. p. 110.

[45] *VI*, p. 170.

[46] See Waldenfels' in "The Paradox of Expression," p. 99.

[47] *PP*, p. 380.

[48] Benjamin, "The Image of Proust," p. 202.

[49] ". . . all images are polysemous; they imply, underlying their signifiers, a 'floating chain' of signified, the reader able to choose some and ignore others. Polysemy poses a question of meaning and this question always comes through as a dysfunction, even if this dysfunction is recuperated by society as a tragic (silent, God provides no possibility of choosing between signs) or a poetic (the panic 'shudder of meaning of the Ancient Greeks) game; in the cinema itself, traumatic images are bound up with an uncertainty (an anxiety) concerning the meaning of objects or attitudes. Hence in every society various techniques are developed intended to *fix* the floating chain of signifieds in such a way as to counter the terror of uncertain signs; the linguistic message is one of these techniques. At the level of the literal message, the text replies—in a more or less direct, more or less partial manner—the question: what is it? the text helps to identify purely and simply the elements of the scene and the scene itself; it is a matter of denoted description of the image (a description which is often incomplete) or, in Hjelmslev's terminology, of an *operation* (as opposed to connotation). The denominative function corresponds exactly to an *anchorage* of all the possible (denoted) meanings of the object by recourse to a nomenclature." Barthes, Roland (1988) *Image-Music-Text*, translated by Stephen Heath. New York: Noonday Press, pp. 38–9.

[50] *VI*, p. 153.

[51] Blanchot, Maurice (2003) *The Book to Come*, translated by Charlotte Mandell. Stanford: Stanford University Press, p. 14.

[52] ibid.

[53] *VI*, p. 150.

[54] Freud, Sigmund (1964) "Writers and Day-Dreaming," in *The Standard Edition of the Complete Psychological Works of Sigmund Freud vol. 14*, translated under the general editorship of James Strachey. London: Hogarth Press, pp. 134, 135.

[55] Merleau-Ponty, Maurice (1970) *In Praise of Philosophy and Other Essays* (Henceforth referred to as *IPP*), translated by John O'Neill. Evanston: Northwestern University Press, p. 109.

56 ibid.

57 Proust, *Remembrance of Things Past*, p. 204.

58 *IPP*, p. 110.

59 ibid.

60 ibid., p. 109.

61 ibid., p. 110.

62 ibid.

63 ibid.

64 ibid.

65 Dillon, M. C. (2001) *Beyond Romance*. Albany: State University of New York Press. p. 134.

Chapter 4

1 *PrP*, p. 184.

2 *VI*, p. 7.

3 ibid., p. 9.

4 ibid., pp. 7 and 8.

5 ibid., p. 6.

6 ibid., p. 8.

7 ibid., p. 7.

8 ibid., p. 8.

9 ibid., p. 7.

10 ibid. p. 8.

11 ibid., p. 9

12 *PrP*, p. 167.

13 Ibid.

14 Bernet, Rudolf (1999) "The Phenomenon of the Gaze in Merleau-Ponty and Lacan," in *Chiasmi International Vol. 1*. Paris: Librarie Philosophique J. VRIN, p 115.

15 Lawlor, Leonard "Introduction" to *HLP*, p. xxii; quote originally found in Bibliotèque Nationale, 43.

16 *VI*, p. 190.

17 Watson, Stephen H. (2009) *Crescent Moon over the Rational: Philosophical Interpretations of Paul Klee*. Stanford: Stanford University Press, p. 23.

18 Johnson, *The Retrieval of the Beautiful*, p. 154.

19 Lawlor, "Introduction" to *HLP*, p. xxiii, quote originally found in Bibliotèque Nationale 40, 43.

20 Heidegger, Martin (1992) *Parmenides*, translated by André Schuwer and Richard Rojcewicz. Indianapolis: Indiana University Press, p. 84.

21 ibid., p. 85.

22 ibid.

23 ibid., p. 84.

24 ibid., p .85.

25 ibid.

26 ibid., p. 79.

27 ibid., p. 80.

[28] Mallarmé, Stéphane (1982) *Selected Poetry and Prose*, translated by Mary Ann Caws. New York: New Direction Books, p. 77.

[29] Nancy, *Corpus*, p. 17,

[30] The third page begins with the tentative phrase "*SOIT que*" and though he begins his text on the conventional left-hand page, Mallarmé also retreats to lower-case type. The tentative "*SOIT que*" and the introduction of an emptiness, "*L'Abime*" mark a fading from the force of the poet's earlier statement, "*JAMAIS*," which appears only after a long hesitation on the second page. The poem, in its retreat from the "*JAMAIS*" and into the fading "*L'Abime*," threatens a total cancellation by the white page itself. It reveals to us that all poems are on the verge of falling to their surplus. But they do not hide this immanent failure. Mallarmé, Stephane (1914) "Un coup de Dés jamais n'abolira le Hasard". Paris: La Nouvelle Revue Française, 1914, pp. 4–5.

[31] Lacoue-Labarthe, Philippe (1999) *Poetry as Experience*, translated by Andrea Tarnowski. Stanford: Stanford University Press, p. 19.

[32] ibid.

[33] Apollinaire, Guillaume, "The New Painting: Art Notes" in *Art in Theory 1900–2000*, p. 188.

[34] Ladnowska, Janina, "Katarzyna Kobro: A Sculptor of Space" in *Artibus et Historiae*, Vol. 22, 2001, p. 178.

[35] ibid.

[36] ibid.

[37] Sartre, Jean-Paul (1988) "The Quest for the Absolute" in *Essays in Existentialism*. New York: Citadel Press, p. 396.

[38] ibid.

[39] Cleaver, Dale, "The Concept of Time in Modern Sculpture" in *Art Journal* Vol. 22, 1963, p. 234.

[40] ibid.

[41] Husserl, Edmund (1997) *Thing and Space Lectures of 1907*, translated by Richard Rojcewicz. Dordrecht: Springer, p. 101.

[42] *HLP*, p. 117.

[43] *PrP*, p. 185.

[44] Grosskurth, Brian (2006) "Inside-Out: Rebecca Horn's Extimate Monument" in *Sculpture and Psychoanalysis*. Aldershot: Ashgate Publishing, p. 180.

[45] ibid., p. 179.

[46] ibid. In architecture, according to Lacan, the void is central and constitutes its "true meaning." Lacan spends a good portion of time examining temples, palaces, houses, etc., as meaning an unrepresentable core of absence. He goes so far as to extend this to the history of prehistoric art. Cave paintings, for example, were done in caves that were unlit – interior spaces that were empty, occupied only by *das Ding*. See Lacan, Jacques (1992) *The Ethics of Psychoanalysis 1959–1960*, translated by Dennis Porter. New York: Norton & Company, Inc., pp. 136–42.

[47] Ponge, Francis, "Reflections on the Statuettes, Figures and Paintings of Alberto Giacometti" in *Art in Theory 1900–2000*, p. 625.

[48] *PrP*, p. 123.

[49] ibid., p. 146.

[50] Agamben, Giorgio (1999) *The End of the Poem*, translated by Daniel Heller-Roazen. Stanford: Stanford University Press, pp. 110–11.
[51] ibid., p. 109 and 113.
[52] ibid., p. 113.
[53] *VI*, p. 155.
[54] ibid.
[55] ibid., p. 144.
[56] ibid. p. 151.
[57] ibid., p. 243.
[58] *N*, p. 46.
[59] *VI*, p. 151.
[60] ibid., p. 144
[61] ibid.
[62] ibid.

Concluding Remarks

[1] *VI*, p. 148.
[2] ibid.
[3] ibid.
[4] ibid.
[5] ibid.
[6] ibid.
[7] ibid., p. 148–9.
[8] Husserl, *Ideas I*, pp. 167–71.
[9] ibid., p. 169.
[10] ibid., p. 156.
[11] ibid.
[12] ibid.
[13] ibid. For an illuminating reflection on these same passages, see also Kohak, Erazim V. (1980) *Idea and Experience: Husserl's project in Ideas I*. Chicago: University of Chicago Press. Especially the chapter "Hermeneutics and the Return to Phenomenology."
[14] ibid.
[15] Mishara, Aaron L. (1990) "Husserl and Freud: Time, Memory and the Unconscious." *Husserl Studies* 7: pp. 38–9.
[16] Elkins, *What Painting Is*, p. 5.
[17] Welish, Marjorie (1999) *Signifying Art: Essays on Art After 1960*. Cambridge: Cambridge University Press, p. 35.
[18] ibid.

Bibliography

Agamben, Giorgio (1999) *The End of the Poem*, translated by Daniel Heller-Roazen. Stanford: Stanford University Press.

Apollinaire, Guillaume, "The New Painting: Art Notes" in *Art in Theory 1900–2000*: an anthology of changing ideas, edited by Charles Harrison and James Wood. London: Blackwell Publishing. pp. 187–8.

Aristotle (1996) *Metaphysics, Books I–IX*, translated by Hugh Tredennick. Cambridge: Harvard University Press.

—(1996) *The Physics, Books I–IV*, translated by F. M. Cornford and P. H. Wickseed. Cambridge: Harvard University Press.

Barbaras, Renaud (2005) *Desire and Distance: Introduction to Phenomenology of Perception*, translated by Paul Milan. Stanford: Stanford University Press.

—(2009) *Le tournant de l'experience*. Paris: VRIN.

Barthes, Roland (1988) *Image-Music-Text*, translated by Stephen Heath. New York: Noonday Press.

Biemel, Walter "Zu Marcel Proust, Die Zeit als Hauptperson," *Philosophische Analysen zur Kunst der Gegenwart, Phaenomenologica* 28, 1968.

Blanchot, Maurice (2003) *The Book to Come*, translated by Charlotte Mandell. Stanford: Stanford University Press.

Benjamin, Walter (1968) "The Image of Proust" in *Illuminations: Essays and Reflections*. New York: Pantheon Books, pp. 203–17.

Bernet, Rudolf (1999) "The Phenomenon of the Gaze in Merleau-Ponty and Lacan" in *Chiasmi International Vol. 1*. Paris: Librarie Philosophique J. VRIN, pp. 105–20.

Bollas, Christopher (2008) *The Evocative Object World*. London: Routledge.

Breeur, Roland (2000) *Singularité et sujet. Une lecture phénoménologique de Proust*. Paris: Jérôme Millon.

Carbone, Mauro (2004) *The Thinking of the Sensible: Merleau-Ponty's A-Philosophy*. Evanston: Northwestern University Press.

Casey, Edward S. (2000) *Remembering: A Phenomenological Study*. Bloomington: Indiana State University.

Cleaver, Dale, "The Concept of Time in Modern Sculpture," *Art Journal* vol. 22, 1963, 232–36.

Crowther, Paul (2009) *Phenomenology of the Visual Arts (even the frame)*. Stanford: Stanford University Press.

Deleuze, Gilles (2004) *Proust and Signs*. Minneapolis: University of Minnesota Press.

Dillon, M. C. (1997) *Merleau-Ponty's Ontology, 2nd Edition*. Evanston: Northwestern University Press.

—(2001) *Beyond Romance*. Albany: State University of New York Press.

Dufrenne, Mikel (1981) "Eye and Mind" in *Merleau-Ponty: Perception, Structure, Language*, edited by John Sallis. Atlantic Highlands: Humanities Press, pp.167–73.
—(1987) *L'oeil et l'oreille.* Montreal: Éditions de l'Hexagone.
—(1990) *In the Presence of the Sensuous: Essays in Aesthetics.* Amherst, New York: Prometheus Books.
Elkins, James (2000) *What Painting Is.* London: Routledge Press.
Flam, Jack (1995) *Matisse on Art.* Los Angeles: University of California Press.
Foucault, Michel (1971) *The Order of Things: An Archeology of the Human Sciences.* New York: Pantheon.
Freud, Sigmund (1964) "Writers and Day-Dreaming" in *The Standard Edition of the Complete Psychological Works of Sigmund Freud vol. 14*, translated under the general editorship of James Strachey. London: Hogarth Press, pp.143–53.
Gaschet, Rudolf (1997) "Alongside the Horizon" in *On Jean-Luc Nancy: The Sense of Philosophy*, edited by Darren Sheppard, Simon Sparks and Colin Thomas. London: Routledge, pp. 136–51.
Genette, Gérard, "Métonymie chez Proust," *Figures* vol. 3, 1972, 41–63.
Greenberg, Clement (1993) *The Collected Essays and Criticism*, vol. 4, edited by John O'Brian. Chicago: University of Chicago Press.
Grosskurth, Brian (2006) "Inside-Out: Rebecca Horn's Extimate Monument" in *Sculpture and Psychoanalysis.* Aldershot: Ashgate Publishing, pp. 177–94.
Haar, Michel (1999) *La philosophie français entre phénoménologie et métaphysique.* Paris: Presses Universitaires de France.
Hart, James G., "Toward a Phenomenology of Nostalgia" in *Man and World: An International Philosophical Review*, vol. 6, 1973, 397–420.
Hegel, G. W. F. (1975) *Hegel's Aesthetics: Lectures on Fine Arts Vol. II*, translated by T. M. Knox. Oxford: Oxford University Press.
Heidegger, Martin (1953) *Einführung in die Metaphysik.* Tübingen: Niemeyer.
—(1962) *Being and Time*, translated by John Macquarrie and Edward Robinson. New York: Harper & Row Publishers.
—(1964) *Lettre Sur L'humanisme, Suivi D'une Lettre à Monsier Beaufret*, translated by R. Munier. Paris: Aubier.
—(1975) *Gesamtausgabe* vol. 9, entitled *Wegmarken*, edited by Friedrich-wilhelm von Herrmann. Franfkfurt am Main: Vittorio Klostermann.
—(1975) "Origins of the Work of Art" in *Poetry, Language, Thought*, translated by Albert Hofstadter. New York: Harper & Row.
—(1992) *Parmenides*, translated by André Schuwer and Richard Rojcewicz. Indianapolis: Indiana University Press.
Husserl, Edmund (1940) "Grundlegende Untersuchungen zum phänomologischen Ursprung der Räumlichkeit der Natur" in *Philosophical Essays in Memory of Edmund Husserl.* Cambridge: Harvard University Press, p. 324.
—(1983) *Ideas Pertaining to a Pure Phenomenology and to a Phenomenological Philosophy: First Book: General Introduction to a Pure Phenomenology*, translated by Fred Kersten. Dordrecht: Springer.
—(1997) *Thing and Space Lectures of 1907*, translated by Richard Rojcewicz. Dordrecht: Springer.
Jay, Martin (1993), *Downcast Eyes: The Denigration of Vision in 20th-Century French Thought.* Berkeley and Los Angeles: University of California Press.

Johnson, Galen (2000) "Thinking in Color: Merleau-Ponty and Paul Klee" in *Merleau-Ponty: Difference, Materiality, Painting*, edited by Veronique M. Foti. Amherst: Humanity Books, pp. 169–176.

—(2010) *The Retrieval of the Beautiful: Thinking Through Merleau-Ponty's Aesthetics.* Evanston: Northwestern University Press.

Klee, Paul (1993) *On Modern Art* in *Art in Theory, 1900–2000: An Anthology of Changing Ideas*, edited by Charles Harrison and James Wood. London: Blackwell Publishing, pp. 362–9.

Kohak, Erazim V. (1980) *Idea and Experience: Husserl's Project in Ideas I.* Chicago: University of Chicago Press.

Kristeva, Julia (1993) *Proust and the Sense of Time*, translated by Stephen Bann. London: Faber and Faber Limited.

Lacan, Jacques (1992) *The Ethics of Psychoanalysis 1959–1960*, translated by Dennis Porter. New York: Norton & Company, Inc.

Lacoue-Labarthe, Philippe (1999) *Poetry as Experience*, translated by Andrea Tarnowski. Stanford: Stanford University Press.

Ladnowska, Janina, "Katarzyna Kobro: A Sculptor of Space" *Artibus et Historiae*, vol. 22, 2001, 161–85.

Lingis, Alphonso (1969) "The Elemental Background" in *New Essays in Phenomenology*, edited by James M. Edie. Chicago: Quadrangle Books, pp. 24–38.

Lyotard, Jean-François (1994) *Lessons on the Analytic of the Sublime*, translated by Elizabeth Rottenberg. Stanford: Stanford University.

—(2001) *Soundproof Room: Malraux's Anti-Aesthetics*, translated by Robert Harvey. Stanford: Stanford University Press.

—(2002), *Discours, Figure*. Paris: Klincksieck Press.

Mallarmé, Stéphane (1982) *Selected Poetry and Prose*, translated by Mary Ann Caws. New York: New Direction Books.

Malraux, André (1990) *The Voices of Silence*, translated by Stuart Gilbert. New Jersey: Princeton University Press.

Martin, David, "On Perceiving Paintings and Sculpture" *Leonardo* vol. 11, 1978, 287–92.

Ménasé, Stéphanie (2003) *Passivité et création: Merleau-Ponty et l'art moderne*. Paris: Presses Universitaires de France.

Merleau-Ponty, Maurice (1964) *Sense and Nonsense*, translated by Hubert L. Dreyfus and Patricia Allen Dreyfus. Evanston: Northwestern University Press

—(1964) *Signs*, translated by Richard C. McCleary. Evanston: Northwestern University Press.

—(1964) *Primacy of Perception and Other Essays*, edited by James E. Edie. Evanston: Northwestern University Press

—(1968) *The Visible and the Invisible*, translated by Alphonso Lingis. Evanston: Northwestern University Press

—(1970) *In Praise of Philosophy and Other Essays*, translated by John O'Neill. Evanston: Northwestern University Press.

—(1970) *Themes from Lectures at the Collège de France 1952–1960*, translated by John O'Neill. Evanston: Northwestern Press.

—(1973) *Prose of the World*, translated by John O'Neill. Evanston: Northwestern University Press, 1973.

—(1988) "Philosophy and Non-Philosophy Since Hegel" in *Philosophy and Non-philosophy since Merleau-Ponty*, edited by Hugh J. Silverman. London: Routledge, pp. 9–78.

—(2003) *L'institution et la passivité: Notes de cours au Collège de France*. Paris: Editions Belin.

—(2003) *Nature: Course Notes from the Collège de France*, translated by Robert Vallier. Evanston: Northwestern University Press.

—(2003) *Phenomenology of Perception*, translated by Colin Smith. London: Routledge Press.

—(2004) *The World of Perception*, translated by Oliver Davis. London: Routledge.

—(2007) *Husserl at the Limits of Phenomenology*, edited by Leonard Lawlor and Bettina Bergo. Evanston: Northwestern University.

—(2008) "La Nature ou le monde du silence" in *Maurice Merleau-Ponty*, edited by Emmanuel de Saint Aubert. Paris: Hermann Éditeurs, pp. 41–53.

Mishara, Aaron L. (1990) "Husserl and Freud: Time, Memory and the Unconscious." *Husserl Studies*, vol 7, 29–58.

Morrison, James, and Stack, George J., "Proust and Phenomenology" in *Man and World: An International Philosophical Review*, vol. 1, November 1968, 604–17.

Nancy, Jean-Luc (1993) *The Birth to Presence*. Stanford: Stanford University Press.

—(1996) *The Muses*, translated by Peggy Kamuf. Stanford: Stanford University Press.

—(2008) *Corpus*, translated by Richard A. Rand. New York: Fordham University Press.

Paz, Octavio (1990) *The Collected Poems of Octavio Paz, 1957–1987*. New York: New Direction Books.

Ponge, Francis, "Reflections on the Statuettes, Figures and Paintings of Alberto Giacometti" in *Art in Theory 1900–2000*: an anthology of changing ideas, edited by Charles Harrison and James Wood. London: Blackwell Publishing. pp. 625–6.

Proust, Marcel (1998) *Remembrance of Things Past: Book 1 Swann's Way*, translated by Terence Kilmartin and C. K. Scott Moncrieff. New York: Penguin Classics.

Richardson, William J. (1973) *Heidegger: Through Phenomenology to Thought*. Reinbek: Rowohlt.

Russon, John (2007) "The Spatiality of Self-Consciousness: Originary Passivity in Kant, Merleau-Ponty and Derrida" in *Chiasmi International Vol. 9*. Memphis: University of Memphis Press, pp. 219–32.

Sartre, Jean-Paul (1988) "The Quest for the Absolute" in *Essays in Existentialism*. New York: Citadel Press, pp. 388–401.

Slatman, Jenny (2003) *L'expression au delà de la representation: Sur l'aisthêsis et l'esthétique chez Merleau-Ponty*. Leuven: Peeters-VRIN.

Steinbock, Anthony J. (2000) "Reflections on Earth and World: Merleau-Ponty's Project of Transcendental History and Transcendental Geology" in *Merleau-Ponty: Difference, Materiality, Painting*, edited by Veronique M. Foti. Amherst: Humanity Books, pp. 90–111.

Taminiaux, Jacques (1981) "From Dialectics to Hyperdialectics," in *Merleau-Ponty: Perception, Structure, Language*, edited by John Sallis. Atlantic Highlands: Humanities Press, pp. 58–76.

Vallier, Robert (2006) "Institution: The Significance of Merleau-Ponty's 1954 Lectures at the Collège de France" in *Chiasmi International Vol. 7*. Memphis: University of Memphis Press, pp. 281–302.

Visker, Rudi (1999) *Truth and Singularity: Taking Foucault into Phenomenology*. Dordrecht: Kluwer Academic Publishers.

Waldenfels, Bernard (1996) *Order in the Twilight*, translated by David J. Parent. Athens: Ohio University Press.

—(2000) "The Paradox of Expression" in *Chiasms: Merleau-Ponty's Notion of Flesh*, edited by Fred Evans and Leonard Lawlor. Albany: State University of New York Press, pp. 89–102.

Watson, Stephen, H. (2009) *Crescent Moon over the Rational: Philosophical Interpretations of Paul Klee*. Stanford: Stanford University Press.

—(2009) *In the Shadow of Phenomenology: Writings After Merleau-Ponty I*. London: Continuum Books.

Welish, Marjorie (1999) *Signifying Art: Essays on Art After 1960*. Cambridge: Cambridge University Press.

Wölfflin, Heinrich (1950) *The Principles of Art History: The Problem of the Development of Style in Later Art*. Mineola, New York: Dover Publications.

Index

abstract expressionism 7
aesthetic, the 2, 6, 7, 10–11, 21, 36,
    38, 50, 51, 56, 58, 86
    aisthēsis 51–2
Agamben, Giorgio 26, 126
Aristotle 81

Barthes, Roland 106
Basquiat, Jean-Michel 116
Benjamin, Walter 94, 106
Blanchot, Maurice 17, 25, 108
Breton, André 7

Cage, John 128
cave painting 17, 31, 51–3, 55–7,
    61–2
    Lascaux 17, 26, 31, 51, 55, 56
Cézanne, Paul 3, 4, 20, 78, 80, 88,
    117, 124
codex 25
colour 21, 36, 46, 54–5, 61, 69, 70,
    72, 77–81, 117, 122
    the rhythm of 77
    colouration 46, 54–5, 77, 78,
    80–1
cubism 87, 121

da Vinci, Leonardo 75
    childhood memories and 85
desire 11, 23, 24, 62, 70, 75, 81–3,
    87, 88–92, 95–6, 100, 102, 103,
    108, 109, 114, 115, 124
    "labour of" 24, 25, 82
    natural being and 83
Dufrenne, Mikel 12, 47, 68

Earth 21, 45, 46, 51, 53, 59–60, 69,
    123
    as ground 21, 45, 51, 53, 55, 59, 60
    as *Ur-Arché* 21, 45, 51, 124
Ernst, Max 12
"exscription" 26
expression 8, 10, 18, 19, 20, 21, 25,
    28, 30, 31, 34–7, 39, 40, 44, 46,
    47–51, 53, 59, 67–8, 76, 78, 92,
    102–3, 109, 127
    gesture and 7, 18, 47, 49, 50
    institution and 18, 47–9
    the paradox of 34, 48, 102
expressionism 46

figurative, the 25, 112–15, 117, 129,
    130
figuration 114, 115, 119, 120, 129
"figured philosophy" 113
flesh 19
    "the flesh of history" 20, 43, 46
    the reversibility of 25
Freud, Sigmund 85, 86, 91, 92, 108

Giacometti, Alberto 122, 125
Goya, Francisco 83

hearing 35, 68, 104, 127, 129, 130
Hegel, G. W. F. 40–3, 53, 72, 74, 82
Heidegger, Martin 21, 22, 34, 60,
    63–7, 105, 117, 118
Henry, Michel 55
history 7, 12, 20, 21, 28–31, 40–6,
    52, 55, 60, 63, 102
    "flesh of" 20, 43, 46

horizon 8, 9, 10, 11, 16, 17, 24, 45,
    53–5, 59, 61, 98
    see also world
Husserl, Edmund 1, 13, 20, 32,
    44, 45, 51, 59, 66, 81, 97, 103,
    123, 127
hyper-dialectic 5, 6, 11, 18, 42

imaginary space 38, 49, 50, 108
impressionism 46
inscription 17, 26, 45, 46, 115,
    118–20, 125, 129
    inscribing hand 26, 118
    see also "exscription"
institution 1, 2, 3, 12, 13, 14, 15, 16,
    18, 19, 20, 27, 46–9, 50, 89, 93, 95
    expression and 18, 46, 47–9
    as *Stiftung* 1, 44, 48, 93
    as *UrStiftung* 1, 13, 44, 45, 90,
    94, 109

Klee, Paul 72, 77, 78, 80, 81, 88,
    116, 117
Kristeva, Julia 102

Lacan, Jacques 124
Lacoue-Labarthe, Philippe 119
language 25, 28, 29, 30, 31–6, 37,
    39, 40, 55–6, 60, 73, 102, 107,
    116, 117, 118, 119, 125–7
light 57, 63, 64, 70, 74–5, 80, 83,
    86, 87
    and the concept of *lumen* 73
    and the concept of *lux* 74
line 21, 26, 29–30, 36, 38, 40, 55,
    61, 70, 75–9, 84, 87, 112–13,
    115, 117, 121
    grapheme 75
Lyotard, Jean-François 47, 86, 87, 91

Magritte, René 36
Mallarmé, Stéphane 26, 39, 119,
    120, 125

Malraux, André 30, 31, 40, 41, 42, 43
Matisse, Henri 18, 28, 29–31,
    37–40, 49, 50, 71, 77, 112–13
matter 50, 51, 57, 61, 62
    extension 51, 61
    mass 56, 57
meaning 4, 9, 14, 23, 26, 31–5, 37,
    39, 47–8, 52, 54–5, 62, 65–7, 68,
    70, 73, 78, 80–7, 90, 93–6, 98,
    99, 100, 101, 103–4, 105–9, 111,
    115–17, 119, 121, 126, 127
    expression and 9, 33, 34, 68, 87
    the origin of 14, 104, 120, 127
mimēsis 7, 8, 16, 50, 115, 117, 120
    see also representation
music 107, 115, 125, 127, 129

Nancy, Jean-Luc 49, 52–5, 57, 119
Nature 6, 7, 10, 13, 14, 47, 55, 60–1,
    63, 67, 68, 70, 79, 80, 86, 121
    natural being 5, 6, 7, 11, 22, 23, 51,
    57–8, 60–2, 65, 70, 71, 81–3, 87
    see also physis

ontological difference 3, 16, 18, 20,
    43, 60, 63, 67
    differentiation 6, 10, 11, 17,
    24–6, 60–1, 65–7, 121
    Heidegger and 63
    natural being in Merleau-Ponty
    and 20, 60, 67
    physis in Heidegger and 63

perspective 4, 7, 70–5, 121
phonemic oppositions 33, 35,
physis 22, 23, 24, 57, 58, 60, 63–5, 67
Picasso, Pablo 86, 87
picture plane 122
    planarity 26, 56, 57, 75, 76
poetry 12, 115, 120
Ponge, Francis 125
Proust, Marcel 24, 25, 62, 90,
    93–102, 104–11, 116, 120, 128

representation 8, 10, 12, 16, 17, 44, 54, 56, 83, 85, 112, 122
  see also mimēsis

Sartre, Jean-Paul 19, 82, 122
Saussure, Ferdinand de 32–3, 34, 35, 37, 107
sculpture 26, 115, 121, 122, 124, 129
sense 5, 12, 16, 26, 32, 35, 39, 51, 92, 99, 107, 109, 111, 116, 119, 120, 126, 127, 128
  linguistic sign and 32, 127
  noema and 32, 127
  see also sign
"secret science" 6
significance 62, 84, 89, 90
sign 13, 29, 30, 31–6, 37, 39, 107, 108
  linguistic sign 30, 31–6, 37, 107, 126
silence 35–6, 86, 107, 125, 126, 127, 129
  language and 35–6, 40, 126
  painting and 48
  "the mute arts" 129
sound 26, 125, 126, 127, 128, 129, 130
  sounding 33, 115, 125–30
  see also hearing, music speech
space 3, 4, 9, 16, 17, 18, 19, 20, 26, 27, 30, 31, 36, 38, 39, 40, 44, 45, 47, 49, 50, 52, 53, 56, 59, 70, 71, 72–6, 79, 81, 86, 102, 121–5, 128, 129, 130
"spatial spread" 20, 21, 26
  spatial being 20, 121
  spatiality 21, 25, 26
speech 35, 117, 126, 127
  speaking 126
  see also phonemic oppositions
style 12, 19, 20, 21, 31, 40, 41, 44, 51, 52, 80
  of being 19, 20, 46, 48, 58,
  of the gesture 46, 58, 82

of the painter 19, 20, 31, 40, 41, 43, 48, 82
surrealism 7

temporality 14, 15, 16, 45, 66, 84, 89, 91, 92, 96, 98, 102, 111, 116, 123
  consciousness and 66, 92, 97, 102
touch 17, 19, 51, 52, 53, 57, 61, 62, 80, 84, 120, 122, 128
  tangibility 17, 25, 125
  the tangible 25, 84, 125, 128
  touching 17, 19, 121
text 25, 26, 36, 95, 106–9, 116, 117, 119–20, 125–6
  the literary work of art 25, 116
  and Proust 25, 116
  and the white page 119–20
Twombly, Cy 138

vision 4, 6, 8, 9, 10, 12, 13, 16, 17, 25, 36, 41, 56, 64, 79, 86, 113, 125
  horizon and 10
  passivity and 8, 13
  labour of 113
voice 127–8
vocifera tion 129

Wölfflin, Heinrich 56, 57
world 4, 8, 9, 10, 11, 13, 14, 16, 19, 24, 30–1, 34–5, 38, 45–9, 51–9, 62, 66, 72–3, 74–6, 78–9, 81, 83, 86, 88, 89, 103 104, 105, 108, 113–14, 117–18, 125, 127
  being-in-the-world 53
  historical world 46
  life-world 45
  world-as-horizon 45, 53, 59
  world-ray 73, 74
writing 26, 36, 108, 116–18
  see also the codex, inscription, inscribing hand text